Game Production

Game Production

Prototyping and Producing
Your Board Game

Geoffrey Engelstein

CRC Press
Taylor & Francis Group
Boca Raton London New York

CRC Press is an imprint of the
Taylor & Francis Group, an **informa** business

first edition published 2021
by CRC Press
6000 Broken Sound Parkway NW, Suite 300, Boca Raton, FL 33487-2742

and by CRC Press
2 Park Square, Milton Park, Abingdon, Oxon, OX14 4RN

© 2021 Taylor & Francis Group, LLC

CRC Press is an imprint of Taylor & Francis Group, LLC

ISBN: 978-0-367-62690-7 (hbk)
ISBN: 978-0-367-52774-7 (pbk)
ISBN: 978-0-367-62690-7 (ebk)

Typeset in Minion
by Deanta Global Publishing Services, Chennai, India

Contents

SECTION II   **The Development Lifecycle**

About the Author

Geoffrey Engelstein is the designer of many tabletop games, including The Ares Project, the Space Cadets series, The Dragon & Flagon, and The Expanse. He is the founder of Ludology, a bi-weekly podcast about game design, and a contributor to the Dice Tower podcast with his bi-weekly GameTek segments that discuss the math, science, and psychology of games. He has also published several books, including *GameTek: The Math and Science of Gaming*, *Achievement Relocked: Loss Aversion and Game Design*, and *Building Blocks of Tabletop Game Design*. He is on the faculty of the NYU Game Center as an adjunct professor for Board Game Design and has been invited to speak at PAX, GenCon, Metatopia, and the Game Developers Conference.

Introduction

WE ARE IN A golden age for tabletop games. (In this book we use the term "tabletop game" to include both board and card games.) There are thousands of new games published each year, and more and more people are participating in the hobby. Television shows like *Hollywood Game Night*, The Big Bang Theory, and even Saturday Night Live prominently feature tabletop games. The movie *Game Night* grossed more than $117.6 million and *Battleship* over $303 million. And new games like Catan, Codenames, Pandemic, Cards against Humanity, and Wingspan have broken through into wide public awareness and popularity.

With that popularity, more people have gotten the design bug, and worked on their own creations. Game design is a fantastic outlet for creativity, as it comes at the intersection of many disciplines – math, psychology, art, and graphic design just to name a few. And like engineering projects, the designer is subject to constraints that make the development process incredibly challenging. Designers need to balance rules complexity, play time, component count, product cost, and more. It is a pursuit that can be an incredibly satisfying career or hobby.

Another factor in the rise of tabletop games is Kickstarter. In 2019, tabletop games raised over $170 million, a 7% increase over 2018, and represented over 30% of the total money raised by Kickstarter for the year. Tabletop games are truly the engine that drives Kickstarter.

Because gamers are used to looking for new projects on Kickstarter, it has become a viable way for new designers to turn their dream into a reality. The gatekeeping of publishers and distributors no longer stand in the way of new games reaching fruition. Kickstarter allows individuals and publishers to go directly to the game-playing public.

This book is not about how to design a game, or how to test, iterate, and polish it. There are a number of terrific books that cover those topics, including *Building Blocks of Tabletop Game Design* (CRC Press, 2019) written by myself and Isaac Shalev, and Tracy Fullerton's *Game Design Workshop* (CRC Press, 2018).

This book is about the physical craft of putting together a game. Board and card games are physical objects that must be manipulated by the players. Cards need to be laid out and printed. Fonts and colors need to be decided on. Rules need to be laid out. And the preparation of those objects throughout the design cycle can be daunting. New designers in particular often spend an inordinate amount of time on the physical preparation of prototypes and production samples, unaware of tricks and techniques that can dramatically streamline this process.

This book is in two major sections. The first covers general topics in prototyping and production, while the second goes through the life cycle of game development, and different techniques that are required for each stage

PART I: GENERAL TOPICS

Chapter 1: Tools of the Trade

This chapter covers the materials, physical tools, and software that is helpful to have available at all times, to allow you to rapidly get just about any design to a playable state.

Chapter 2: Graphic Design

Here we discuss the graphic elements of your design. How do you use fonts, colors, and shapes effectively to allow the players to easily understand the rules? What are the guidelines for designing iconography? And how can you maximize usability so that your game is accessible to as wide an audience as possible?

Chapter 3: Writing Rules

Rules are the "original sin" of tabletop games. Before being able to start, players must wade through and grasp the rules. If your rules are badly laid out or hard to understand, it may turn off players before they even complete turn one. This chapter lays out best practices on rules writing and layout, how to make effective illustrations, and more.

PART II: THE DEVELOPMENT LIFECYCLE

Chapter 4: Alpha Prototypes

The key to early-stage testing is to be able to iterate on prototypes quickly. If you're anything like 99% of game designers, your first prototypes will be terrible. So investing as little time as possible into them and rapidly creating the next version is incredibly important to maintaining your design momentum. This chapter gives helpful tips on how to quickly make cards, boards, tokens, and more.

Chapter 5: Beta Prototypes

Once your design is more mature you can switch to beta prototypes. Here, your purpose is to streamline usability, draw players into the theme, and make sure your game is easy to learn. These require an elevated prototype and some new techniques.

Chapter 6: Production

If you are going to publish the game yourself, it is critical to understand how to work with your printer – what types of files they want, how to deal with bleed and color matching, die lines for punchboard, and more. Even if you are planning to license the game to another publisher, having a grasp on the realities of printing and component cost can help you make your design more amenable to a potential publisher. Going in to a pitch being able to explain not just why your game is great, but also why it will be economical to produce is a big plus.

Chapter 7: Conclusion

This chapter contains some final tips, as well as giving some big picture suggestions. There is also a list of online resources for the topics discussed in this book.

I

General Topics

CHAPTER 1

Tools of the Trade

RAPID PROTOTYPE KIT

This book is not about where to get ideas from, and how to design your game. It's about the physical parts of your game – prototyping, layout, and production. But if you're new to game design, I'll tell you one thing about the design process: You'll get lots of ideas, and more as you become more experienced. I'm sure the experienced game designers reading this will agree.

When those ideas hit, when inspiration strikes, you should have a notepad or list on your computer or someplace where you store them. But many ideas will have a way of worming their way into your brain, and demand to be tested.

You need the ability to try out these ideas as quickly as possible. And for that I highly recommend that you invest in a Rapid Prototype Kit. This is a set of core components that you can grab and use to quickly make mockups for your ideas.

If you're anything like me, you'll find out pretty quickly that most of your ideas don't have any merit – at least not initially. But the fastest way to figure that out is to make a quick prototype and push some pieces around.

Having a kit like this will give you options to rapidly test and discard ideas. If you have to order specific components to try out an idea, you'll become more invested in it, which can be an issue when it turns out that the idea is not that great. The more you're invested in an idea, both emotionally and financially, the harder it will be to let it go. Being able to just grab stuff you already have and try something out will make it easy to move on, and just put the materials back into your box.

Here are the core items you want to have at your fingertips:

Index Cards

Index cards are the backbone of your development kit. They are incredibly versatile, as you can use them for cards, tokens, player mats, tiles, and even standees.

Sticking with the classic 3″ × 5″ index card (metric A7) is good for a number of reasons. First, they are the least expensive. A thousand blank index cards can be had for about $10 and will last quite a while. Unlined are also preferred, as the lines typically go unused for a normal game prototype.

Second, half an index card (3″ × 2.5″) is very close to the size of a standard playing card, which is 3.5″ × 2.5″. Personally, I use index cards as is, and don't worry about cutting them in half. However, the option is there, and they will fit well into sleeves (see "Penny Sleeves" section).

Of course, index cards are designed to just be scribbled on, and not fed through your printer, so you won't be getting high quality output. However, sitting with a stack of index cards and colored markers can be a terrific brainstorming tool. The physical act of scribbling card ideas on the index cards, even in the middle of a playtest, can be very useful for rapidly generating ideas.

Index cards also are a quick and easy way to make standees. If you cut a strip the short way and fold it in half, you'll get a piece that is about 1.5″ tall, an excellent height for a standee. It can either be used as is on the table (like a tent) or finished with a binder clip (see the Standee section in Chapter 4 for full details).

And, of course, don't limit yourself to white. Having a variety of different colors will make it easy to prototype different card decks, tokens, or other objects.

Dice

There are two broad categories of dice that you should have in your toolkit: with numbers and blank.

For any design that uses dice, traditional dice with pips or numbers should be your first stop, even if you envision custom symbols or sides. We'll talk more about this in Chapter 4, but in general you should want to get into testing as quickly as possible. Determine if you're even in the ballpark of a workable design before spending time stickering blank dice.

Bulk six-sided dice are relatively inexpensive. Get them in sets of various colors. This gives more design flexibility than just buying a ton of white dice. A set of 100 in various colors typically costs around $10–$15. Similarly, sets of polyhedral dice (D4–D20) typically cost around $10 for seven sets of different colors when bought in bulk. Do a search for "bulk dice" on online retailers or educational supply sites to locate these.

Blank dice can also be purchased in a variety of colors, although white is typically the least expensive. Fifty blank white dice cost about $10 versus $15 for a pack of 50 dice with a variety of colors. Depending on your application, you may be able to use white dice and put color on the sticker. Blank polyhedral dice are also available, but given the smaller triangular or pentagonal facets, it can be challenging to sticker them properly.

The above pricing for blank dice is for traditional smooth-surfaced dice. There is another variety of blank dice called *indented dice*. These have an indent on each face to place a sticker of your custom design. The advantage of indented dice is that the raised edges protect the stickers from wear. If you are rolling stickered dice frequently, you will notice significant wear. For early testing, this is not an issue, but some designers prefer better aesthetics once they get into beta prototypes and publisher presentations. If you don't want to sticker a fresh set of dice for these occasions, you may consider indented dice. However, be aware that they are more expensive and larger than traditional dice (Figure 1.1).

Cubes

It is always valuable to have a large supply of cubes on hand. They can act as markers, money, resources, workers, and a host of other functions. It's great to have an assortment of different colors for different players or different representations.

The least expensive source for cubes is to purchase *centimeter cubes* (so-called because, not surprisingly, they measure 1 cm on each side – a shade under 1/2″). One thousand centimeter cubes in various colors cost around $20. These are readily available from traditional online retailers and educational supply stores.

If you prefer the feel or aesthetics of *wooden cubes*, these are actually a bit tricky to buy in bulk. The best sources I've found are board game prototypers like The Game Crafter and Print Play Productions. In these sites,

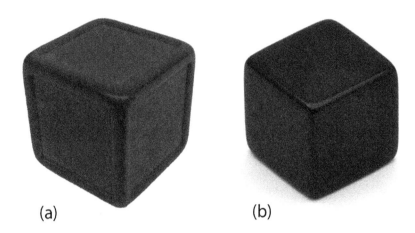

(a)   (b)

FIGURE 1.1   Indented (a) and smooth (b) blank dice

look for bulk packages to get the best deals. The website Spielematerial.de in Germany also has great prices and selection, but you need to order enough to make the shipping worthwhile.

Regardless of where you order them from, wooden cubes are going to be much more expensive than centimeter cubes – about $100 per 1,000 rather than $20.

Penny Sleeves

Penny Sleeves are inexpensive card sleeves that are transparent on both sides. They get their name from their cost, which is usually around $0.01 each, but the price will vary widely based on the quantities purchased.

Plastic Tiles

To complement your centimeter cubes, it may also be worthwhile investing in a bucket of plastic tiles. These tiles are 1″ × 1″ and have a nice chunky feel. The cost of 400 of these in various colors is around $15. Not as critical as having cubes around, but I find myself dipping into this bucket when working on a prototype very frequently (Figure 1.2).

SPECIALTY COMPONENTS

There are a variety of components that are nice to have available, but tend to be more specialized in their application, or are more useful when making better quality prototypes (what we refer to here as *beta prototypes*).

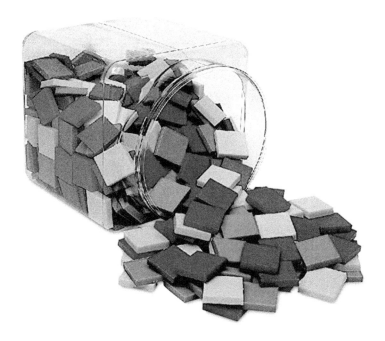

FIGURE 1.2   Plastic tiles

Full-sheet Labels

Having a pack of full-sheet labels is invaluable. These can be used for creating boards, tiles, dice, and more. A pack of 100 sheets costs about $10–$15. Although office stores typically carry many varieties of labels, the brick-and-mortar locations usually do not have full-sheet labels. I speak from experience after making a last-minute dash around town one evening before a game design conference. However, they are readily available online at office supply stores and with most major retailers.

Chipboard

To go with the full-sheet labels, you should have a supply of 8.5″ × 11″ chipboard sheets. With the application of a full-sheet label, these are the basis for your boards and tokens.

You will typically see these offered in two thicknesses: 0.022″ or 0.030″, sometimes referred to as "22 point" and "30 point." The heavier material is stiffer and will withstand more handling but is more expensive and a bit harder to cut.

Hexagonal, Circular, and Square Tiles

Game prototype houses like the aforementioned Game Crafter, Print Play Productions, and Spielmaterial have blank white hexagons, squares, and circles of various sizes. If you are making a more polished prototype, you will typically use the full-sheet label/chipboard technique discussed in Chapter 4. But early on it can be helpful to be able to grab a bunch of blank tiles and just scribble on them to try out an idea. However, this can often be done with index cards as well, which is why these are in the "nice to have" category.

Meeples

While cubes can substitute for meeples through much of a design cycle, if you wish to use actual meeples in your game, you can get a set of 100 in 10 different colors for about $10. So it's not a huge investment if you like the visual appeal.

Binder Clips

Small binder clips seem like an unlikely resource for the game designer, but there are two main use cases.

First, they can be invaluable for creating standees. I go into this method in more detail in Chapter 5.

Second, if you print your board on paper or cardstock, you can use binder clips to attach it to an existing game board. This is quick, temporary, and much less messy than using spray adhesive or other glue.

Stealing from Other Games

A great resource for components for your prototype is other games in your collection. Cubes, meeples, dice, tokens, and more can all be "borrowed" from the other games you own. A key suggestion though – particularly as you get more into game design and work on multiple prototypes: leave a note in your games that specifies which components you took and which prototype they are in. You'll be thankful when you pull a game off of the shelf and find half the pieces missing!

PHYSICAL TOOLS

In addition to having a supply of materials, you will need a core set of tools to be able to assemble prototypes. Here we discuss the core tools and some tips about how to get the best results:

- Cork-backed steel ruler

- Box cutter knife

- Self-healing cutting mat

These three tools are used together to cut cardstock, index cards, and paper.

There are a wide variety of box cutters available, and a trip to your local hardware or craft store should yield a wide selection. Personally, I prefer the style with snap-off blades over replaceable blades, but replaceable blades will give you a cleaner and more consistent cut.

While any straight edge can be used to make straight cuts, a steel ruler with a cork backing won't slip during use and won't scratch your surface of what you're cutting.

To prevent scratching the surface you are cutting on, it is worth investing in a decent self-healing cutting mat. They are called "self-healing" because over time the surface will become smooth again after being scratched by the blade. This will give you a good, consistent work surface. Cutting mats also typically have grids, rules, angles, and other features printed on them to help you align features. If you are cutting cards that only have crop marks on the outer edges of the page rather than full outlines, having the grid and ruler on the cutting mat can be vital for keeping everything consistently sized (Figure 1.3).

Cutting Tips

Cutting cardstock with these tools is straightforward; however, there are a few considerations. First, you don't need that much pressure to cut, particularly if you are working with a sharp blade.

The fastest approach is to do all cuts of the same orientation in sequence and then rotate sheet. For example, when cutting a 3 × 3 sheet of cards, do all four vertical cuts first, then rotate and do the four horizontal cuts. Sometimes cardstock will get stuck to the cutting mat, particularly if you are cutting out small components like tokens, so it may be quicker to rotate the mat rather than peel off the paper and rotate it.

When cutting, do not cut all the way to the edge if possible. This will make it faster since you can continue to work on the same sheet rather than have separate strips that may shift or come off the cutting mat. However, if you are cutting small components like tokens, it can sometimes be quicker

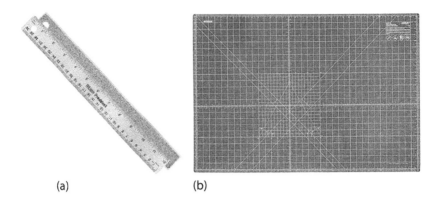

(a)   (b)

FIGURE 1.3   Steel Ruler (a) and Cutting Mat (b)

to cut out full strips and then trim off the components using a scissor to simply snip them off the strip.

It is recommended to only cut a single sheet at a time. If you stack sheets it can be difficult to keep them aligned, as they will want to slide against each other, and you will not cut the lower sheets as accurately. If you're feeling the urge to cut multiple sheets at once, invest in a flatbed rotary trimmer.

If you are folding your cardstock (to make standees or 3D elements, for example), you should score the fold lines while you are trimming. To create a score, lightly drag the knife across the cardstock. Apply hardly any pressure. You are simply trying to break the top surface of the paper. Scoring will give you much cleaner folds.

Handheld Rotary Cutter

If cutting out a large number of cards, some prefer to use a handheld rotary cutter. These can cut faster and have less chance of tearing the cardstock since they are rolling instead of slicing. You should still use a steel ruler to ensure a straight cut, however.

The disadvantage of the handheld rotary cutter is that it is more challenging to start a cut at a precise location. For example, if you are cutting out hexagonal tiles, it will be next to impossible to use a rotary cutter to get a clean cut at the corners of the pieces. A box cutter should be used in these cases (Figure 1.4).

Flatbed Rotary Trimmer

A flatbed rotary trimmer excels at cutting out sheets of cards and tokens. While a straight edge and box cutter can do everything a rotary cutter can

FIGURE 1.4   Handheld rotary cutter

do, the rotary trimmer will be much faster and more efficient. You will spend at least 75% less time cutting cards with a flatbed rotary trimmer.

Because this is such an important tool, I recommend investing in a heavy duty rotary Trimmer like the one pictured in Figure 1.5.

To use this, place the cardstock on the bed and line up the cutting edge with the line you want to cut. Then you secure the clamp and slide the rotary blade up and down. Because the blade is constrained to run along the cutting edge you can move the blade much more quickly than you can with a box cutter or handheld rotary cutter.

Because the sheets are held with a clamp, you can cut up to four or five sheets with this style of cutter. This alone makes for a huge timesaver. If you are cutting multiple sheets, make sure to align them by tapping them against the table and then force the stack against a guide rail to keep it aligned and straight while applying the clamp.

The first few times you use it, a flatbed rotary trimmer may seem like more trouble than it's worth. But once you get in the rhythm, you'll find it an indispensable part of your game prototyping arsenal.

Printer

Once you get past the hand-scribbled notecard step, you are going to need a printer to output your game materials. When printer shopping, here are some things to keep in mind.

FIGURE 1.5 Flatbed rotary trimmer

Inkjet versus Laser

One of the first decisions you'll need to make to narrow down your options is whether to get an inkjet or a laser printer. Here are the key differences:

- Inkjets have lower up-front costs but are more costly to operate in the long term. They also tend to take up less space on your desk.

- Lasers will give you crisper text, while inkjets will produce more vibrant colors.

Ensure that the printer you choose can print 50 kg cardstock. Most can, but some of the more compact inkjets may have difficulty routing the paper if it makes a sharp bend.

If it is in your budget, having a printer that can do duplex printing (double side) will be a real plus. Not having to feed the sheets back in again to print the other side speeds up the process, prevents alignment issues, and makes sure the orientation is correct.

CNC Cutter

If you're doing a lot of cutting, particularly odd shapes, it might be worthwhile to invest in a computer-controlled cutter. With a CNC (Computer Numerical Control) Cutter, you load the material on a sticky sheet to hold it down and then upload a pattern from your computer or a USB stick to the machine telling it where to cut. Then you just have to step back and watch the magic happen.

CNC Cutters can cut through cardstock, chipboard, and even fabric. If you're cutting irregular shapes, curves, or even basic shapes like hexagons or circles, the cuts will be a lot sharper and more precise. However, they do only cut a single sheet at a time, so for basic card cuts, using a flatbed rotary trimmer will be more efficient.

There are some neat features of CNC Cutters that you may find attractive. First, you can substitute a pen in for the blade and draw designs on the material, and then switch to a blade to cut. You can also define certain lines to be scored, rather than cut, so if you are doing complex folding shapes, this machine will be much more efficient.

The downside, of course, is the price. The Cricut Maker and Brother ScanNCut are two of the more popular models and cost between $300 and $400, although you can sometimes find sales for an even lower price. (I was able to obtain a ScanNCut for about $270.)

The ScanNCut has an additional feature which you can probably guess from the name – a built-in scanner. Rather than uploading the cutting lines, it can scan the sheet, find the edges of objects, and then cut around them. You will need to make sure that there is sufficient white space around your objects for the scanner to identify them, and may have to take a few minutes to delete any stray marks the scanner picked up that you don't want cut. However, it's a bit magical when you simply print a bunch of interestingly shaped tokens on a label sheet, stick it on chipboard, and then put it into the cutter and a few minutes later have a set of beautifully cut tokens ready to go.

Spray Adhesive

Spray adhesive can be used to attach paper and cardstock to chipboard, foam core, and other backing materials. Many designers prefer printing onto full-sheet labels and then sticking them to the backing, but this is an alternative. There are a few advantages of using spray adhesive. First, it is less expensive. Full-sheet labels are quite a bit more costly than cardstock or paper sheets. Second, it can be used with larger sheets. Full-sheet labels are only readily available in 8.5″ × 11″ size. So if you want to use a single sheet that is larger than that (a 14″ × 14″ board, for example), you will have to do it with multiple labels, which can create alignment, durability, and aesthetic issues. If you are doing large format printing at, say, a copy shop, you can use spray adhesive to back it yourself.

When using spray adhesive, it is important to follow the instructions on the can. Make sure you are working in a well-ventilated area, as the fumes can be dangerous. When attaching the paper to the backing, start by placing one corner and then gradually working your way out. Make sure to smooth out bubbles as you work.

Most spray adhesives are "repositionable." This means that you have a short period of time from when you place the paper to pull it back up if it is not aligned properly.

Corner Punch

A Corner Punch, or Corner Rounder, is used, not surprisingly, to round the corners on cards and tokens. This will give your components a more finished appearance, but is not really necessary for prototypes, particularly in the early stage. It will reduce the chances that cards will have bent corners and make them easier to shuffle. But if you are using a penny-sleeve method, these are not really considerations. See Chapter 4 for more details about card making.

Laminator

Laminating can be useful for protecting components like player boards and reference cards. They are also useful if you are creating components to be written on and erased. I personally do not laminate prototypes for durability. I have only used one when creating a roll and write game and wanted to be able to test repeatedly on the same sheet by being able to erase it.

Laminators are not expensive – a basic one goes for approximately $25. It is not a large investment if you prefer the finished look that they can give you. Note that it is not advisable to laminate cards if they need to be shuffled. Use Penny Sleeves instead. Chapter 4 has more details about how to make cards.

Circular Punch/Hex Punch

If you are making many smaller tokens that are circles or hexagons, it may be worthwhile to invest in a punch. These can quickly pop tokens out of a sheet of cardstock, saving much time over using a box cutter or pair of scissors, and give you much more consistent and professional results.

A punch costs between $10 and $20.

SOFTWARE TOOLS

There is a wide variety of software tools that can help with tabletop game development. They have a wide range of use cases, capabilities, and costs. In this section, we survey some of the more popular tools available.

Almost all of these packages have some sort of free trial available. It is always worth testing something out before spending money, to get a feel for how it works and how it fits into your working process.

Regardless of which software you end up using, I strongly recommend sticking with it and becoming an expert in it. Flitting back and forth between packages and jumping to the latest neat thing will slow you down and actually end up reducing productivity. In my work, for example, I've used Adobe Illustrator for years, and the keyboard shortcuts, like using ALT to copy-drag something, which have become second nature, make it very easy for me to whip up a quick prototype. All tools have their short-cuts and quirks. Only by sticking with it will you learn how to make it work for you.

Vector Drawing

Vector drawing software is ideal for creating cards, boards, diagrams, and other elements for games. It is called "vector" drawing because it is based around lines and shapes and their mathematical description, not the underlying pixels. This means that enlarging shapes will not result in the jaggedness that you can get with bitmap or photo editing software.

It also means that the core elements of basic tabletop game design – shapes and lines with different fills and colors and text at different sizes and angles – are the sweet spots of these programs. Vector drawing most naturally flows into the bulk of prototype design work.

Here are some contenders in this category:

Adobe Illustrator

Illustrator is part of the Adobe Creative Cloud package. It is the industry standard and natively produces AI and PDF files, which any production house will be able to handle. It also interoperates (mostly) seamlessly with its Creative Cloud siblings, Photoshop and InDesign, which makes it simple to, for example, include Illustrator files of diagrams into an InDesign rulebook layout. And because it is so popular, there are many tutorials and resources online.

It is, however, by far the most expensive option discussed here. It is only available through a monthly subscription. There are discounts for students and teachers, and it is less expensive for individuals than businesses, but it is still an investment. Sometimes if you are associated with a university or other educational institution, you may be able to get a heavily discounted version.

Inkscape

Inkscape is a free open source vector drawing program that is a credible alternative to Illustrator. It is not as polished, and is not updated as frequently, but if you are using core functionality – and most likely for game design you will – then Inkscape can do an excellent job. Given the cost, it's certainly worth trying out to see if it meets your needs.

Affinity Designer

The Affinity family of products, from Serif, are very polished, mid- to high-end programs that do most of what the Adobe family can do at a fraction of the price. While not free, like the open source packages mentioned, Affinity just requires a one-time purchase and not a subscription like Adobe.

Google Draw

Google has an online drawing package called Google Draw. It is free with a Google account and has the advantage that multiple people can easily work on the same document. The drawing tools are not nearly as robust as the others discussed here, but it is constantly being upgraded and improved and might prove useful in certain applications.

Microsoft Office

The Microsoft Office family of products – Word and Excel being the most well known – contain vector drawing tools. I know people that use Excel to create cards, player aids, and other game elements. Typically, this is done by shrinking rows and columns and using data-driven formulas to create the elements. Conditional Formulas can be used to color cells and elements. Similarly, Word can be used via the Table option to create grids of cards. Word also has the capability to do mail merge (discussed later this chapter in the section Mail Merging Workflow.), which will allow to maintain a spreadsheet with card data which is used to populate card templates.

However, in general, it has similar limitations to Excel, making it more challenging to lay out elements in the precise way you envision.

If you are comfortable with Excel or Word, sticking with Microsoft Office might be an option. However, ultimately it can be fiddly and challenging to get the results you envision (Figure 1.6).

Image Editing

Sometimes called "Art," "Painting," or "Photo Editing" software, Image Editing software is primarily designed to work on a pixel level. Although there are almost always tools to draw polygons and text, they are not typically set up to handle them as smoothly as vector drawing programs.

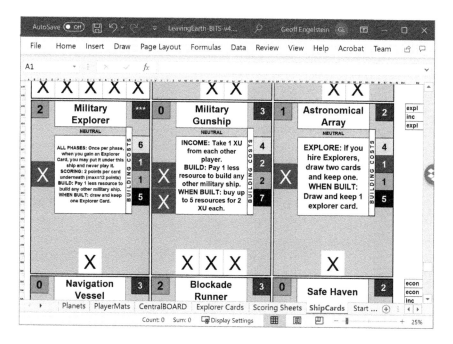

FIGURE 1.6 Prototype cards in Excel for Leaving Earth (Fatula, 2015). (Courtesy of Joseph Fatula.)

Therefore, Image Editing software is not typically used for prototypes. However, if unlike me you are skilled enough to create your own production-level artwork for final release, then these tools will be invaluable.

Adobe Photoshop

As with many Adobe products, Photoshop is both the industry standard in this category and the most expensive. If you have a subscription to Illustrator, you most likely will have access to Photoshop as well.

GIMP

First released in 1995, GIMP is a free, open source image editor. It is extremely powerful and can handle all but the most demanding projects.

Affinity Photo

Like Affinity Designer, Affinity Photo is a much less expensive alternative to Photoshop with a one-time purchase cost.

Page Layout

Document layout software is primarily used for creation of rulebooks, guides, scenario books, and similar. Some versions can also do a "mail merge" or "data merge" that allow the use of a spreadsheet to create a series of similar elements like cards or tiles.

Microsoft Word

Word and other basic word processors (like Google Docs) are fine for creating alpha and beta rulebooks. If you are going to be laying out final rules yourself, you will find that the limitations of laying out diagrams, sidebars, glossaries, and other common rule elements will tax traditional word processing software to the limit. You will be much better served using page layout software.

Adobe InDesign

InDesign is the page layout member of the Adobe Creative Suite. As such, it comes with strong features and a price to match. However, it will allow you to achieve just about any effect on a page. It also has very strong mail merge capabilities, which will allow you to create cards, tokens, and other repetitive elements based on data in a spreadsheet.

Scribus

Scribus is a free, open source page layout program. For some functionality that you may want, like mail merge, it relies on external python scripts. Therefore, it is a little bit more challenging to use.

Affinity Publisher

Like Affinity Designer and Photo, Affinity Publisher is a much less expensive alternative to InDesign with a one-time purchase cost.

Specialized Software

As board games become more popular and designers more numerous, several software tools that are specifically designed for tabletop games have emerged.

nanDECK

nanDECK is software that is designed to help generate cards, tiles, and tokens. It is free, and has been actively developed and supported for many years. It is available at www.nand.it/nanDECK

nanDECK is best described as a scripting language. To create a deck of cards, for example, you write a series of instructions that tells the software what the cards should look like, how many of each, and other features. The listing below shows a sample script. When you run your script, nanDECK will turn it into a PDF or series of images.

```
cards = 18
border = rectangle
font = arial, 28, B, #0000FF
text = "1", "SEER", 0, 3, 6, 3, center
font = arial, 28, B, #FF0000
text = "2-4", "WEREWOLF", 0, 3, 6, 3, center
font = arial, 28, B, #000000
text = "5-18", "VILLAGER", 0, 3, 6, 3, center
```

nanDECK can link to external Excel files, so that you can create a list of the cards you want and their features and easily change them during development. Once you become familiar with the syntax it can be very powerful to easily tweak values or formats and update card appearance and style.

The downside is that there is a learning curve to the syntax. The latest versions have included a graphic studio that shows you previews of your cards and checks for errors in your script. Coders will certainly be more at home in nanDECK and pick it up quicker. We will go into detail on creating a nanDECK script later in this chapter so that you can get a better idea of the process.

nanDECK can export data in a format targeted to The Game Crafter and Tabletop Simulator, which can be a shortcut if you are using them for beta prototypes.

Component.Studio

Component.Studio is a relatively new entrant in this space and was created by The Game Crafter service. It takes full advantage of modern web techniques and has several positive attributes to facilitate component design.

First, it is structured around mail merge. You start by creating or uploading a dataset into the system that contains columns with your card, token, or tile information. You then layout the graphic look of the card by adding elements like text boxes, graphics, and more.

The dataset file, graphics, and icons that you incorporate can all be located on the web and incorporated directly via URL. This makes it easier for multiple people to simultaneously work on the same project, or for working via different computers.

And while they require learning some scripting commands, Component. Studio includes features like inline icons and conditional rendering that give flexibility to the design and layout.

Finally, if you are using The Game Crafter to create your beta prototypes (see Chapter 5 for more details), like nanDECK you can transfer data directly from Component.Studio to The Game Crafter for prototypes. It also includes templates for all the standard card sizes, tokens, and tiles that they offer.

Map Generation Software

Depending on your game, you may consider investigating map generation software. These tools are specifically geared toward making detailed maps, primarily aimed at the role-playing game (RPG) market. The three most popular tools are Campaign Cartographer (www.profantasy.com/products/cc3.asp), Inkarnate (https://inkarnate.com/), and Hexographer (www.hexographer.com/). The last tool specializes in creating hex maps, so if your game is based on a hex field – a wargame, for example – that may be a good option. I recommend using these later in the process for your beta prototypes, when the mechanisms are more stable.

MAIL MERGING WORKFLOW

Mail merge allows you to combine a spreadsheet with a template document to create a series of similar documents, like cards or tiles. It is a very important part of an efficient workflow for the game designer, and so understanding this technique is critical.

In this section, we will look at three programs (InDesign, nanDECK, and Component.Studio) to see how to do a mail merge on each. As an example, we will build prototype cards for my game The Expanse.

These extended examples are not only an introductory instructional guide. They serve to allow you to make a better-informed decision about which of these tools would be the best fit for your process and skill set.

Mail Merge with InDesign

We will be spending a bit more time explaining how InDesign does mail merge to lay out the core concepts, allowing us to simply highlight the differences in the other programs. Note that these instructions and images are for InDesign v15. Your version and exact dialog layouts may vary, but the principles remain the same.

In InDesign the feature is called *Data Merge*. Typically, when you start the process you won't even be in InDesign. You will be in the program that allows you to create a spreadsheet, like Microsoft Excel, or the free Libre Office, Open Office, or Google Sheets.

Each row of your spreadsheet represents one card. Each column represents a piece of information that may change from card to card, like title, cost, or effect.

Figure 1.7 shows part of the spreadsheet that I used for cards for my game The Expanse. There are six columns shown: Card #, Title, Action Pts, 2P, 3P, and Event. The precise details of what these are isn't important. However, briefly, I like to include card number just to make it easier to note cards that might need to be updated from playtesting. "2P" and "3P" mark cards that are used in the 2-player and 3-player games, respectively.

If you have images that are going to change from card to card, it would be great to include that into your spreadsheet as well. Fortunately, all the

A	B	C	D	E	Q
Card #	Title	Action Pts	2P	3P	Event
1	News Feed	2		3	Place 2 influence in the same Base, anywhere you have a fleet.
2	Slingshot Racing	2		3	Remove 1 influence from any Outer Planets Base.
3	Water Riots	3	2	3	Each player scores 2 VP for each controlled Water Base OR Place 1 influence on 2 separate Water Bases.
4	Theresa Yao	3	2		Remove X of your fleets from an Orbital. Remove X+1 opponent fleets (total) from that Orbital. X may be zero.
5	Heavy Burn	3	2	3	Move up to two fleet groups up to two Bands each.
6	Franklin DeGraaf	3	2		Place 1 influence on two different Bases in the Earth Orbital.
7	Food Shortage	3		3	Each player scores 2 VP for each controlled Food Base OR Place 1 influence on 2 separate Food Bases.
8	Black Ops Team	4	2	3	Remove 1 influence from up to 3 bases, each in a different Band.
9	Bobbie Draper	4	2	3	Remove one opposing non-battleship fleet, and place one of your fleets in the same Orbital (either unbuilt, or from another Orbital).
10	Diogo	2			Remove 1 fleet from an Orbital where you have influence on a Base.
11	Asteroid BA-834024112	2		3	Select a Base in the Belt. Move one Influence from each other player from another Belt Base to the chosen Base.
12	Assassin	2	2	3	Each player (including you) must discard one Kept card.
13	Scopuli	2		3	Place 1 influence on each Saturn Base where you do not have influence.
14	Remember the Cant	3			Add up to 3 influence in the Belt, no more than 1 per Base.
15	SematImba	3		3	Remove up to 2 influence from a single Belt Base
16	Drummer	3	2	3	Perform a 1 AP Action.

FIGURE 1.7   Expanse spreadsheet for InDesign

merge programs we will discuss allow you to do that, with different methods. For InDesign, you need to do two things:

- Put an "@" symbol in the header at the start of the name.
- Include the full pathname to the file you want in each row.

For my cards for The Expanse I have an icon that shows who can use the card. It is either "on" or "off" for that faction. If it can't be used, I simply don't want to show any icon. So in my spreadsheet I either include a file-name for the faction icon or leave it blank, so that no icon will be shown. Figure 1.8 shows what this looks like.

Tip: If you have lengthy duplicated entries in your spreadsheet, like the filepath to an image that is on many cards, you may consider using the VLOOKUP function in Excel. This allows you to create a table that has a short code and then the full text that corresponds to it. You can then use a formula in your spreadsheet to populate the field. This way, if you change the file location or name, you only need to change it in the spreadsheet table, and then everything else automatically updates. There are a variety of online resources explaining how to use VLOOKUP and related functions.

One caveat – you should include this table on another sheet in your spreadsheet. This way it will not confuse the export or import program.

Note that you do need headers in your file. You can't just start with the data and assume that the software will know what each column is. Having a header allows InDesign to identify the columns and is required.

Once you create your file, you need to save it in a special format called a CSV file. For Excel, use the File menu, Save As function, and then open

	R	S
1	@MCR	@UN
2	C:\Users\gengelstein\Dropbox\Expanse\MCR.png	C:\Users\gengelstein\Dropbox\Expanse\UN.png
3	C:\Users\gengelstein\Dropbox\Expanse\MCR.png	
4	C:\Users\gengelstein\Dropbox\Expanse\MCR.png	C:\Users\gengelstein\Dropbox\Expanse\UN.png
5	C:\Users\gengelstein\Dropbox\Expanse\MCR.png	
6	C:\Users\gengelstein\Dropbox\Expanse\MCR.png	C:\Users\gengelstein\Dropbox\Expanse\UN.png
7	C:\Users\gengelstein\Dropbox\Expanse\MCR.png	
8	C:\Users\gengelstein\Dropbox\Expanse\MCR.png	C:\Users\gengelstein\Dropbox\Expanse\UN.png
9	C:\Users\gengelstein\Dropbox\Expanse\MCR.png	C:\Users\gengelstein\Dropbox\Expanse\UN.png
10	C:\Users\gengelstein\Dropbox\Expanse\MCR.png	C:\Users\gengelstein\Dropbox\Expanse\UN.png
11		
12	C:\Users\gengelstein\Dropbox\Expanse\MCR.png	
13	C:\Users\gengelstein\Dropbox\Expanse\MCR.png	
14	C:\Users\gengelstein\Dropbox\Expanse\MCR.png	C:\Users\gengelstein\Dropbox\Expanse\UN.png
15		
16		C:\Users\gengelstein\Dropbox\Expanse\UN.png
17		C:\Users\gengelstein\Dropbox\Expanse\UN.png
18	C:\Users\gengelstein\Dropbox\Expanse\MCR.png	
19	C:\Users\gengelstein\Dropbox\Expanse\MCR.png	
20	C:\Users\gengelstein\Dropbox\Expanse\MCR.png	C:\Users\gengelstein\Dropbox\Expanse\UN.png
21	C:\Users\gengelstein\Dropbox\Expanse\MCR.png	
22		C:\Users\gengelstein\Dropbox\Expanse\UN.png
23		
24	C:\Users\gengelstein\Dropbox\Expanse\MCR.png	C:\Users\gengelstein\Dropbox\Expanse\UN.png
25		C:\Users\gengelstein\Dropbox\Expanse\UN.png
26		
27		C:\Users\gengelstein\Dropbox\Expanse\UN.png
28		C:\Users\gengelstein\Dropbox\Expanse\UN.png
29	C:\Users\gengelstein\Dropbox\Expanse\MCR.png	C:\Users\gengelstein\Dropbox\Expanse\UN.png
30		C:\Users\gengelstein\Dropbox\Expanse\UN.png
31	C:\Users\gengelstein\Dropbox\Expanse\MCR.png	C:\Users\gengelstein\Dropbox\Expanse\UN.png

Sheet1 ⊕

FIGURE 1.8 Image columns for InDesign. Note that "@" symbol in the column headers

the file type dropdown under the filename. You'll find CSV file there. It is sometimes called Comma Delimited format (Figure 1.9).

Now you can open InDesign and create your template file. Create a single-page document that is the size that you will be printing on (most likely 8.5″ × 11″ Letter size in North America). Then you need to import the CSV file so that InDesign knows about your fields.

To do this, open the Data Merge tool in the Window/Utilities menu (Figure 1.10). You will see a window as given in Figure 1.11. If you click the "hamburger" icon in the upper right the Data Merge tools menu will pop up. Select Import Data (Figure 1.12), and then you should see your headers in the list box. These are the fields you can use.

↑   📁 C: > Users > gengelstein > Dropbox > (

Expansion Action Cards

CSV UTF-8 (Comma delimited) (*.csv)

Excel Workbook (*.xlsx)

Excel Macro-Enabled Workbook (*.xlsm)

Excel Binary Workbook (*.xlsb)

Excel 97-2003 Workbook (*.xls)

CSV UTF-8 (Comma delimited) (*.csv)

XML Data (*.xml)

Single File Web Page (*.mht, *.mhtml)

FIGURE 1.9   Setting file type when saving in Excel

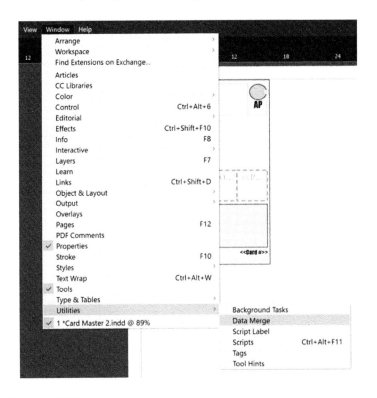

FIGURE 1.10   Utility menu

FIGURE 1.11   Utility window

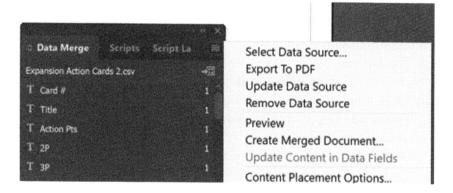

FIGURE 1.12   Import Data

Now you can start laying out the card. Begin by creating a starter rectangle that is the outline of your card. For the layout shown in Figure 1.13, the outer rectangle is 2.5″ × 3.5″, standard Poker size. You then use the standard frame tools to define the locations where fields will be placed. I am not going to teach the basics of InDesign here – there are plenty of resources for how to work with frames and styles. I do recommend that you use Styles to format your fields. It makes it a lot easier to modify the appearance later.

Once you have a frame, you insert the field by dragging and dropping it from the Data Merge panel into the frame. You will then see the

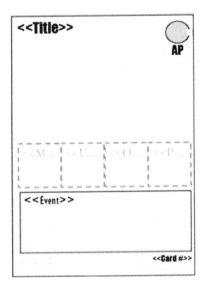

FIGURE 1.13   Template

<<FIELDNAME>> text in the frame showing you that it is placed there. The text will be shown in the Style.

Often, for small fields, you can't see the field name, as it is too long to fit in the frame. For example, the frame that shows the Action Points is in the blue circle. Since it is just a single digit, the text <<Action Pts>> doesn't fit, which is why there is a "+" sign on the frame, indicating that the text is overflowing.

To work with short text, and make sure it looks good, you can turn on Preview in the Data Merge menu (fifth option in Figure 1.12). This will show the actual data in place on the card and can make it much easier to set up your styles and other features. Figure 1.14 shows what the preview for this card looks like. Now you can see the Action Points in the circle.

Preview will also show any image fields which can be helpful to make sure they are sized properly.

Once you have your template set up properly, you can create the merged document. Select "Create Merged Document …" from the Data Merge menu and you will be presented with the options dialog.

Figure 1.15 shows the settings that I use for 2.5″ × 3.5″ cards. The most important is that this is a "Multiple Records" merge. That means that it will place as many copies of the template on a single page as it can, which is what we want for a sheet of cards.

FIGURE 1.14   Preview

The "Multiple Record Layout" tab (Figure 1.15) lets you define margin and put gutters in between the cards on a sheet. I highly recommend leaving the gutters at zero and having the cards butt up against each other. This makes it much quicker to cut them out.

Once everything is set, click OK, and you'll get a new document with the cards laid out, as shown in Figure 1.16. You will also get a message about whether you have any Overset text. If you do, this means that some text did not fit into the frame. You have several ways to deal with this issue:

- Change the template by increasing the frame size or decreasing the font, for example. This will affect all cards.

- Just change the font size in the affected cards. The disadvantage with this is that you will need to apply this fix every time you do a merge.

- Update your source spreadsheet to reduce the amount of text.

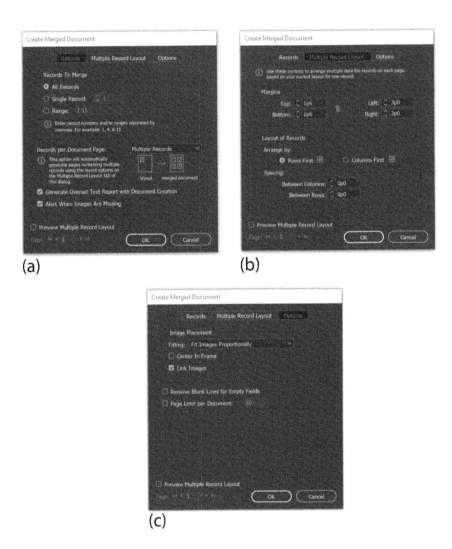

FIGURE 1.15 Multiple Records Settings options

Note that you'll have two documents open in InDesign at this point – the template master and a new document with all the cards. You'll need to save them separately.

If you change the spreadsheet and re-export the CSV file, you will need to select the Update Data Source function on the Data Merge menu to bring the new data into InDesign.

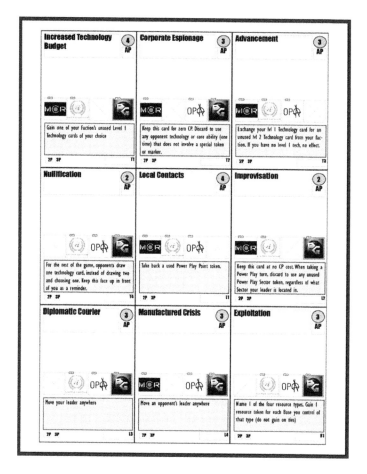

FIGURE 1.16   Final merged document

Mail Merge with nanDECK

nanDECK was released in 2006 and has been continuously updated since then with new features. It has developed a strong community over the years to support new users, which is helpful because it can take a little longer to get going in nanDECK than other programs. However, if you persevere you will find that it is extremely powerful, particularly if you have a coding background.

Unlike the other software discussed in this section, nanDECK is free. InDesign and Component.Studio both have subscription fees.

The basis of nanDECK are scripts – a series of commands that tell it how to create the cards. Here is a very simple sample script to make a deck for Werewolf:

```
cards = 18
border = rectangle
font = arial, 28, B, #0000FF
text = "1", "SEER", 0, 3, 6, 3, center
font = arial, 28, B, #FF0000
text = "2-4", "WEREWOLF", 0, 3, 6, 3, center
font = arial, 28, B, #000000
text = "5-18", "VILLAGER", 0, 3, 6, 3, center
```

The basics of this are relatively easy to follow. There are 18 cards. The first has the text "SEER" in the middle. Cards 2–4 have "WEREWOLF" and 5–18 "VILLAGER." The other elements in each line are parameters that tell nanDECK where to place the text, font size, color, and more.

Fortunately, when you run nanDECK it guides you through each parameter. Figure 1.17 shows how the screen looks like when you run the software.

The script is entered in the large center window. A card preview is shown in the upper right, and diagnostic information is shown in the bottom. This also shows you what are all the parameters that are there for the current command.

One of the advantages of using scripts is that it is easy to share them with other users. This makes it easy to see how other users are accomplishing interesting and powerful effects. It also makes it easier to post your work for others to help debug, or just to help others.

Because of the potential of its scripting language, nanDECK can do some very powerful things. However, it can also do some simple things that are only possible on InDesign and Component.Studio, by jumping through some big hoops. For example, for The Expanse, in addition to the 52 Action cards, there are also six Scoring cards that get shuffled in with the deck. These look nothing like the Action cards – they just say "SCORE" and list the steps for a Scoring phase.

Most mail merge programs want all the cards to look pretty much the same. So if you want to do some cards that are very different in appearance, you either need to make them a separate merge file or just make them by hand in Illustrator or Inkscape (which is what I ended up doing for The Expanse).

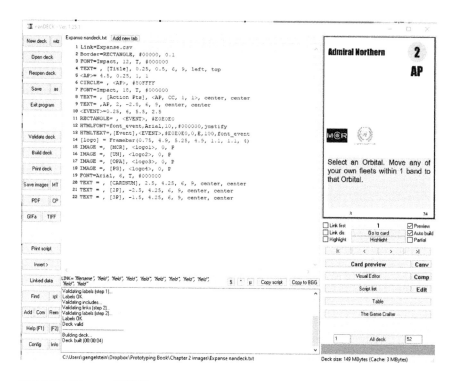

FIGURE 1.17   nanDECK screen

With nanDECK you can just, say, add commands to create additional cards separate from the ones defined by the spreadsheet, the way in which the special SEER and WEREWOLF cards are created above.

Let's take a look at the script to create our prototype cards for The Expanse:

```
Link=Expanse.csv
Border=RECTANGLE, #00000, 0.1
FONT=Impact, 12, T, #000000
TEXT= , [Title], 0.25, 0.5, 6, 9, left, top
<AP>= 4.5, 0.25, 1, 1
CIRCLE= , <AP>, #80FFFF
FONT=Impact, 18, T, #000000
TEXT= , [Action Pts], <AP, CC, 1, 1>, center, center
TEXT= ,AP, 2, -2.8, 6, 9, center, center
<EVENT>=0.25, 6, 5.5, 2.5
RECTANGLE= , <EVENT>, #E0E0E0
FONT=Arial, 12, T, #000000
TEXT=, [Event], <EVENT>, left, wwtop
```

```
[logo] = FRAMEBAR(0.75, 4.9, 5.25, 4.9, 1.1, 1.1, 4)
IMAGE =, [MCR], <logo1>, 0, P
IMAGE =, [UN], <logo2>, 0, P
IMAGE =, [OPA], <logo3>, 0, P
IMAGE =, [PG], <logo4>, 0, P
FONT=Arial, 6, T, #000000
TEXT = , [CARDNUM], 2.5, 4.25, 6, 9, center, center
TEXT = , [2P], -2.5, 4.25, 6, 9, center, center
TEXT = , [3P], -1.5, 4.25, 6, 9, center, center
```

While this may look intimidating, it's pretty straightforward once you understand the syntax. We won't go into everything here, but let's break down the big points.

```
Link=Expanse.csv
Border=RECTANGLE, #00000, 0.1
```

These first two lines give the filename of the CSV file that we are connecting to and tell nanDECK to put a border around the card. #000000 is the color, which is black in this case. nanDECK uses the same syntax as HTML for colors. The six numbers are actually three groups of two digits that define the amount of red, blue, and green in the color.

```
FONT=Impact, 12, T, #000000
TEXT= , [Title], 0.25, 0.5, 6, 9, left, top
```

Here's the title. First, we specify the font and then the text. The text [Title] tells nanDECK that this field is coming from the CSV file – the Title column in this case. The numbers, left, and top define where the text is placed.

That leading comma may look a little odd. The first command in many of these lines lets you tell nanDECK which cards should have that element. If you just wanted the Title on cards 1–10, your line would be:

```
TEXT= 1-10, [Title], 0.25, 0.5, 6, 9, left, top
```

Since most often you want elements on every card, nanDECK has a shortcut. You can leave out the card numbers and just put in the comma. If nanDECK sees that, it knows you want the element on every card.

```
<AP>= 4.5, 0.25, 1, 1
```

This line defines an area on the card where things can be placed and can easily be centered or otherwise lined up. In this case, I want an area for the Action Points so that the blue circle and the number can be easily lined up. I called it AP as a reminder, but that name can be anything.

```
CIRCLE= , <AP>, #80FFFF
FONT=Impact, 18, T, #000000
TEXT= , [Action Pts], <AP, CC, 1, 1>, center, center
```

And here I'm drawing the circle and the text using the AP area. The actual number is pulled from the Action Pts column of the CSV file.

```
TEXT= ,AP, 2, -2.8, 6, 9, center, center
<EVENT>=0.25, 6, 5.5, 2.5
RECTANGLE= , <EVENT>, #E0E0E0
FONT=Arial, 12, T, #000000
TEXT=, [Event], <EVENT>, left, wwtop
```

Next, I do the same thing for the Events. Note that the grey rectangle is drawn first, since nanDECK draws things from top to bottom, so elements that are later in the script will overlay earlier items.

```
[logo] = FRAMEBAR(0.75, 4.9, 5.25, 4.9, 1.1, 1.1, 4)
IMAGE =, [MCR], <logo1>, 0, P
IMAGE =, [UN], <logo2>, 0, P
IMAGE =, [OPA], <logo3>, 0, P
IMAGE =, [PG], <logo4>, 0, P
```

This block draws the four faction icons. The first command – FRAMEBAR – creates a new area on the card. The first numbers define where it is on the card, and the final "4" tells it to break it up into four squares. Then I can drop each icon into its slot. Using FRAMEBAR is nice because it automatically handles placing everything evenly and scaling the images. nanDECK has lots of commands like this that can make complex layouts reasonably easy to achieve.

```
FONT=Arial, 6, T, #000000
TEXT = , [CARDNUM], 2.5, 4.25, 6, 9, center, center
TEXT = , [2P], -2.5, 4.25, 6, 9, center, center
TEXT = , [3P], -1.5, 4.25, 6, 9, center, center
```

And finally, these commands place the card number and 2-player and 3-player indicators at the bottom of the card.

The final output of our script is shown in Figure 1.18:

Once created, these cards can be exported as a PDF file or a series of images.

Mail Merge with Component.Studio

Component.Studio is an online-only tool that was introduced in 2018 by The Game Crafter. It requires a monthly subscription ($10 per month as of this being written).

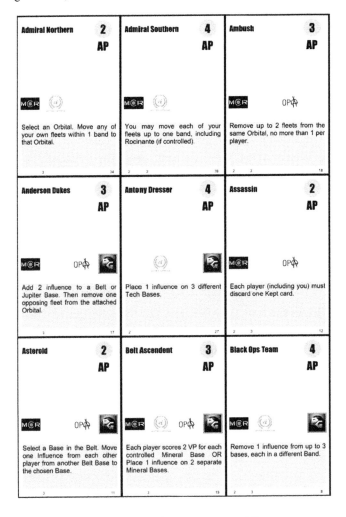

FIGURE 1.18   Expanse prototype cards using nanDECK

We will discuss more about The Game Crafter in Chapter 5, but it is an online resource to create game components of all types. Because Component.Studio is tightly integrated with The Game Crafter, it has built-in templates for their standard cards, tokens, and tiles, but can also do custom sizes. The templates also show "safe zones" for each item. Anything that is outside the safe zone might get cut off due to variation in how cards and tokens are trimmed. Having these right on the card template is a nice touch.

Keep in mind that since it runs in a web browser, you must be connected to the internet to use it. You will not be able to use it if you do not have internet access.

Component.Studio is similar to nanDECK, in that you are creating a series of steps to create the game component. However, where each step in nanDECK is represented by a text script, here it is a web form that you fill in for each step. This makes the learning curve more forgiving than nanDECK.

Typically your first step in Component.Studio, after setting up your account, is to begin a new project and import a data file. You can import a CSV file, as with InDesign and nanDECK, but because it is online you can also connect to a Google Sheet. This makes it much simpler for people to collaborate.

Unlike InDesign and nanDECK, Component.Studio requires that the first two columns be named Quantity and Name, and contain the quantity of that card you'd like, and a unique card identifier. Also, column headers cannot have any spaces in the names.

You don't have to pull data in from a spreadsheet. You can create and edit data sources directly in the web client.

For images, you need to include an online web address to the file. So it must be hosted in Dropbox, Imgur, or similar service. You can also host image files on Component.Studio itself if you'd like.

To prepare the data file for The Expanse cards to work in Component. Studio, I needed to add the Quantity column, renamed Title as Name and moved it to the second column, and renamed Action Pts to ActionPts. I keep the files on Dropbox on Windows, so it is quite easy to get the web address. Simply right-click on the file in Windows Explorer and select Copy Dropbox link and paste it into the CSV file. You can see the "https:\\" prefix showing that it is a web address (Figures 1.19 and 1.20).

Once your dataset is in, you can start laying out the card. This is done by adding a series of objects to the card, which are shown in a list on the

Share...

Send with Transfer...

Copy Dropbox link

Version History

View on Dropbox.com

View Comments

Open in Dropbox

Smart Sync

FIGURE 1.19   Copying the link to a Dropbox file

Edit The Expanse Cards Component Data

quantity	name	Cardnum	ActionPts	2P	3P	MCR	UN	OPA
1	Admiral Northern	34	2		3	https://w	https://w	
1	Admiral Southern	59	4	2	3	https://w	https://w	
1	Ambush	18	5	2	2	https://w		https://w
1	Anderson Dukes	17	3		3	https://w		https://w
1	Antony Dresser	27	4	2			https://w	
1	Assassin	12	2	2	3	https://w		https://w
1	Asteroid	11	2		2	https://w		https://w
1	Belt Ascendent	19	3		3	https://w	https://w	https://w
1	Black Ops Team	8	4	2	3	https://w	https://w	
1	Blockade of Earth	46	3	2	3	https://w		https://w
1	Blockade of Mars	42	3	2	3		https://w	https://w

Add Row   Enumerate On: None   Row Height: 1   non_column_name   Add Column   Remove Column

FIGURE 1.20   Component.Studio dataset

right of the screen. The left shows a preview of the final card. Figure 1.21 shows the objects that are used to create The Expanse prototype card.

The objects are drawn from the top of the list to the bottom. So, if they are in the same space, the later object will hide earlier objects. You'll note that on the sample card the Event Background is higher in the list than the Event Text, since the text should be on top. Same thing with the Action Points Circle and Action Points text.

Figure 1.22 shows the data you need to enter for a text element – in this case, for the Title (which needs to be called *name* in Component.Studio).

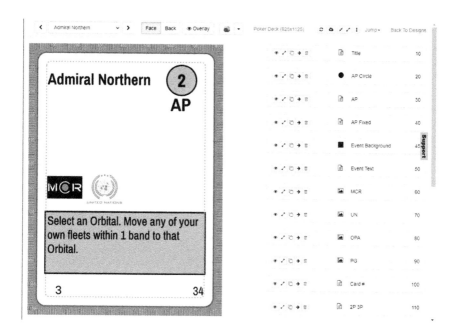

FIGURE 1.21   Expanse card elements in Component.Studio

Figure 1.23 shows the entry fields for an image – in this case, the MCR logo.

For this example, I merely needed to include the field data for the Title and Event. However, Component.Studio has the ability to include markup inside text fields that allows you to do a variety of fancy effects, like including inline icons, having multiple fonts in the same field, and other things that would require a lot of tweaking with other programs. You can also include fields from the dataset in other elements, like color.

Once your design is complete, you can export it from Component. Studio in a variety of ways. As mentioned, you can send it directly to The Game Crafter to have the components created and shipped to you. However, early in your development cycle you probably want to print them yourself. For this you can create PDF files to be printed and cut, or a collection of image files. It also exports in a format ready for Tabletop Simulator, if you are using that tool in your development cycle. Tabletop Simulator is discussed more in Chapter 5 (Figure 1.24).

FIGURE 1.22   Detail of Title element

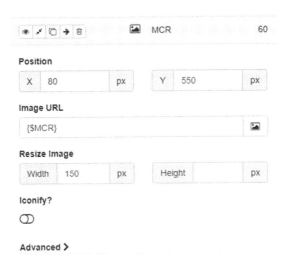

FIGURE 1.23   Detail of MCR logo image

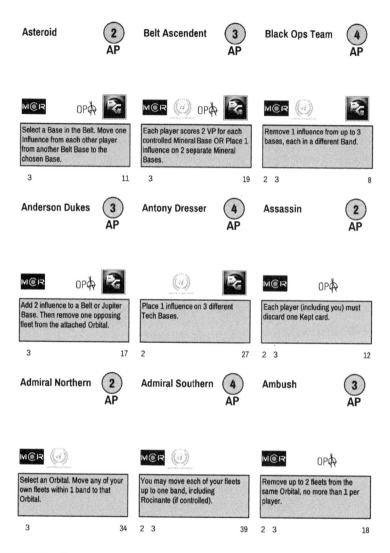

FIGURE 1.24   Expanse prototype cards using Component.Studio

Mail Merge Summary

There are pros and cons to each of the three programs that are discussed here. I am not going to say one is superior to the rest. I know people that are passionately dedicated to each of the tools.

Hopefully one of these spoke to you and seems like something you would be comfortable using. Or perhaps you are torn and not sure which would be the best fit.

Fortunately, all of these tools have free trial versions (or are simply free) that will give you a chance to get hands-on experience with each, so that you can see which you prefer. Regardless of which you select, however, it is important to stick with it and not jump back and forth. Repeated use will allow you to become more comfortable and learn the software's ins and outs.

CHAPTER 2

Graphic Design

WHAT IS GRAPHIC DESIGN?

Graphic design and art are, for the purposes of game design, different things. Graphic design covers the elements that are required by the players to play the game. Art is purely decorative elements, like character images.

As an example, consider the playing card. The main graphic design elements are the card rank and suit in the upper left and lower right corners. The illustration of the Queen is an art element. Other than the spade symbol, and that it is noticeably different than that of Jack or King, the image of the Queen does not impact the gameplay (Figure 2.1).

As another example, a sample production card from The Expanse is presented in Figure 2.2, showing the graphic design elements versus the art. The upper right corner shows the number of Action Points that you gain from using the card. The bottom box shows the effect the card has if it is used as an Event. And the faction flags in the middle show which player factions are allowed to use the Event.

On the very bottom left of the card, there is an indicator showing that this card is used in the 2-and 3-player game.

All of those elements are graphic design elements. They are required to play the game.

There are several artistic elements – the card name in the upper left, the background, and the card image, for example. None of these impacts the play in any way. For most of prototyping these elements can be left off if desired. To the right is the same card from a prototype, which you should be quite familiar with from the previous chapter. While the title was

FIGURE 2.1 The Queen of Spades

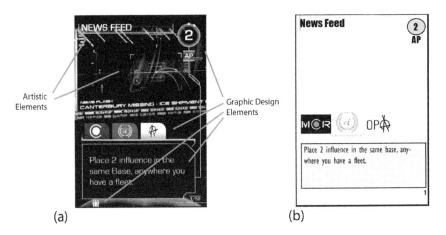

FIGURE 2.2 Production (a) and prototype (b) cards for The Expanse

kept, you'll see that the card is very plain. There's no fancy background (Figure 2.2).

As the designer of the game, you don't have to worry about the art elements. Time spent in art on your prototypes is most likely wasted, particularly if you don't plan on self-publishing. Your game will go through many changes, and art doesn't add a lot until later in development, if at all. We'll talk more about this when we discuss artwork, later in this chapter. The prototype card above is exactly what I submitted to the publisher. I never took the graphic design or art further than this.

While you may not need to focus on the art, you 100% need to focus on the graphic design. Poor graphic design makes a game hard to understand and play and can single-handedly destroy the play experience.

Good graphic design can:

- Make the game easier to learn and play.
- Immerse players in the theme, even without artwork.
- Provide subtle reminders of key rules.
- Prevent mistakes.

When you're doing your earliest prototypes and scribbling on index cards with a marker, graphic design should not be your focus. But the more you work on a design the more attention you should pay to the graphical elements.

Fortunately, creating serviceable graphic design is within the reach of most game designers. A professional graphic designer will be able to elevate your design to the next level, but there's no excuse for any designer to not be able to create a clear and playable prototype.

This chapter will explain the elements of good graphic design, and their relation to specific game elements. We'll conclude with a detailed teardown of Eclipse, an exemplar of great graphic design.

THE THREE READS

At the 2018 Game Developer Conference (GDC), game designer Zach Gage gave a talk titled "Building Games That Can Be Understood at a Glance." You can watch the talk at www.youtube.com/watch?v=YISKcRDcDJg, and I highly recommend it.

In the presentation, Gage introduces a concept called the *Three Reads*. Let's say that you are putting together a concert poster. The most important piece of information is who will be performing. That's the first read. It's large, bold, and can be read from a distance (Figure 2.3).

If you're interested in that, you will read the second tier of information, which probably should include the location and date (Figure 2.4).

Finally, the third read will give you the rest of the details, like the promoter, the precise time, and how to get tickets (Figure 2.5).

Your graphic design creates a *hierarchy* for the player to get oriented. Element size is a great way to create a hierarchy, but it can also be done (or emphasized) with color, or typeface (either a different typeface or using bold or italics).

FIGURE 2.3   First read: performer

FIGURE 2.4   Second read: location and date

For a board game example, let's take a look at Twilight Struggle (Gupta and Matthews, 2005), a simulation of the Cold War. The full board is shown in Figure 2.6. The first read here is that the board is made of boxes connected by lines. In addition, you can tell that the boxes are grouped by geography. There seems to be a Central America group, South America Group, Eastern and Western Europe groups, etc. On the actual color board, this grouping leaps out at you, but even in this grey scale image you can tell these groups apart.

The second read elements are the box headers. Some boxes have white headers, and some headers have a dark background. In the game this is a critical distinction. The boxes with dark headers are *Battleground States*, and those with light backgrounds are *Non-Battleground States*. This distinction is critical for the players. Battleground States are much more

FIGURE 2.5   Third read: ticket price, promoter, and other information

important to control. The use of the dark background for the Battlegrounds is a good choice here. Notice how your eye is immediately drawn to those, due to the contrast between the saturation of the header and box colors.

For the third read on the map boxes, take a look at Figure 2.7, which is a closer look at Europe. Now you can see a few more features of these boxes. First, there is a number in the upper right corner of each box (the Stability number). This is used when resolving certain actions, and while important, it is not as important as the geographic group the box belongs to and whether it is Battleground or not.

Another feature you see on this third read is that each box is divided into two halves, separated by a dashed line. The US and USSR players put influence tokens into these boxes, with the United States placing its tokens

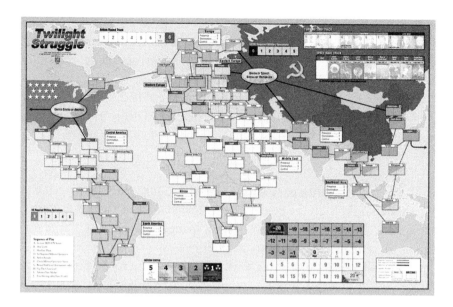

FIGURE 2.6   Twilight Struggle board

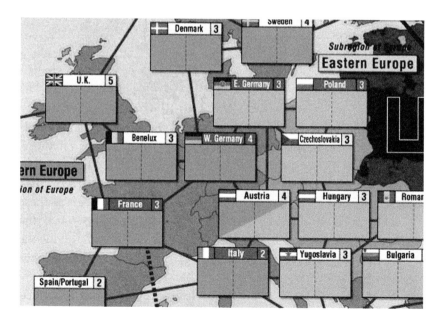

FIGURE 2.7   Close-up of Europe map region

in the left half, and USSR in the right. This is a great example of a design that hints and guides the players, as these squares are the same size as the influence tokens, and the left/right orientation mirrors the placement of the United States and USSR on the map itself.

Creating a consistent hierarchy to orient and guide the player will be a constant theme throughout this chapter. Hierarchy is also critical to creating easily understandable rules, which will be the focus of Chapter 3.

ICONOGRAPHY

Icons have been used in games for more than 5,000 years, going back to the rosette symbols on the board for the Royal Game of Ur that indicated safe spaces. The traditional hearts, clubs, spades, and diamonds on a traditional deck of playing cards are another example.

Almost all games have some form of iconography, as it helps fulfill a number of the goals of graphic design, including differentiating distinct game elements, making the game easier to learn and providing rules reminders.

When you create icons, you are creating a visual language. Like all languages, icons can include game objects (nouns), actions (verbs), and modifiers (adjectives). For example, icons might represent a wood resource (object), drawing a card (action), or increasing a die roll (modifier). You need to look at your icons as a set – a complete language – rather than just evaluating them individually.

Icons should be easily distinguished from the others at a glance. This usually means that icons should be as simple as possible. Do not include unnecessary details. During early prototypes I prefer to use basic shapes (squares, diamonds, triangles, hexagons, etc.) for icons, as they are both very easy to create inside most vector graphics software (see Chapter 1) and very easy to distinguish. Also look for ways to combine simple shapes to create a recognizable shape. For example, a few rectangles and a triangle can quickly be combined to make a sword icon.

If making more complex icons, it is particularly important to take into consideration the distance at which the icons will be viewed and the size they will be printed. If, for example, the icons are on cards that will only be viewed by the owning player in their hand, the icons can be smaller and more detailed. If the card is going to be placed face up in front of the player, and it is important that the other players see and understand the icons from across the table, they will need to be larger and simpler.

We will talk more about color later in this chapter, but this is a good time to mention that color can play a role in distinguishing icons, but it should not play the only role. For example, having red squares, green circles, and blue triangles is a good practice. Having red, green, and blue squares is not.

The icons in Magic: The Gathering (Garfield, 1993) are about as detailed as I would recommend making icons – honestly, they are probably too detailed. At a distance most of the detail will be lost, but there is enough difference in the overall shape/size that they can be distinguished. For example, the white "sun" icon is the only spiky one, and the blue "water" icon clearly takes up the least space in the circle.

While this illustration is not in color, color is used in the game as a secondary identity coding, particularly when viewing at a distance. However, the icons are distinctive even without the color cues (Figure 2.8).

Color and iconography can also subtly distinguish different or special elements in a game. As an example, the game board for Scrabble (Butts, 1948) highlights the special squares as shown in Figure 2.9. Here, the color backgrounds are supplemented by text explaining it. The colors help group similar bonuses – light/dark blue for the double/triple letter scores and light/dark red for the double/triple word scores. The sides of the special squares also have a number of points equal to the bonus (two for double bonus squares and three for triple). These subtle features are not required to be there for the game to work but help to give the player clear signposts about important squares. The points also help the players recognize these important squares even when they are covered by a tile, helping to avoid mistakes while calculating a score.

The game Race for the Galaxy (RftG) (Lehman, 2007) is well known for its extensive iconographic language. Figure 2.10 shows the player aid that explains many of the icons.

RftG illustrates many of the lessons and pitfalls on icon design. First, it is a fairly complex icon system. Most first-time players are overwhelmed

FIGURE 2.8   Magic: The Gathering icons

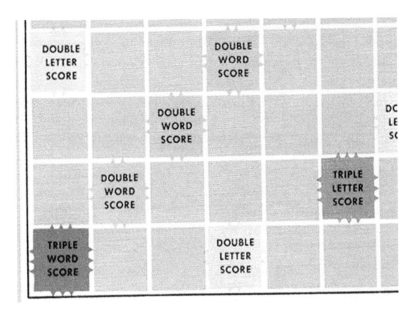

FIGURE 2.9   Scrabble board

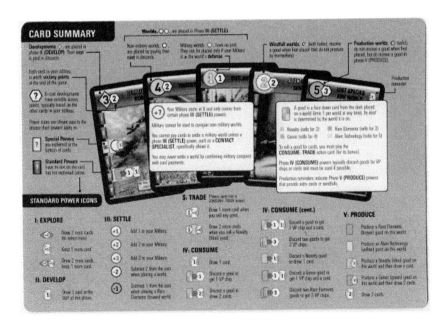

FIGURE 2.10   Reference card from Race for the Galaxy

when being presented with this reference card. However, the consistency and clarity of the icon language makes it much easier for experienced players to understand new cards, or for returning players to pick things back up again. We will discuss more about this dichotomy of teaching new players versus reminding experienced players when we cover rules writing.

Defining the language allows the designer to include a variety of abilities without having to explain each one. For example, Figure 2.11 shows a sample of "consume" abilities. An experienced player will know what these mean due to the consistency of the symbology. The multicolored rectangle means "any resource." A card with a hand on it means "draw a card," and the hexagon means gain that many Victory Points (VPs). The arrow means "spend what's on the left to do what's on the right." So, the

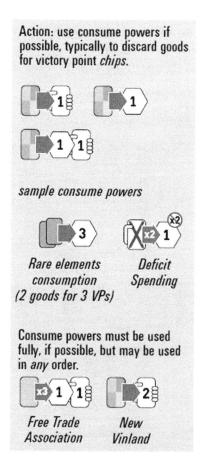

FIGURE 2.11   Race for the Galaxy consume abilities

first group of icons means the player can discard any resource to draw a card. The second means discard any resource for a Victory Point, and the third discard any resource to both draw a card and gain a VP. The final action means discard two brown resources to gain three Victory Points.

Race for the Galaxy has about 12 distinct iconographic elements in its language. This is probably pushing the limit of what is easily understandable without a separate reference guide.

Figure 2.12 shows cards from the game Guilds of London (Boydell, 2016). Here the icons are more "artistic" in style than the Race for the Galaxy icons. There are also more different symbols, as can be seen just from this smattering of sample cards. Because of this, Guilds provides a separate reference sheet that describes the function of all the cards.

Graphic design is sometimes used to achieve language independence. Not having any text on cards and components means that the game is easier to sell in different countries, as only rules and reference sheets need to be changed. However, it is important that the design not make the

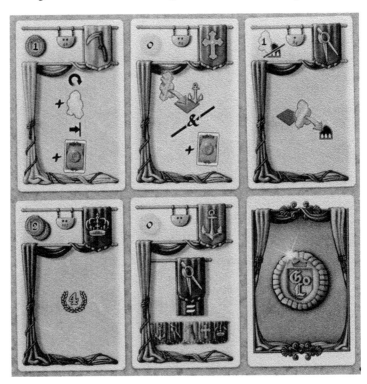

FIGURE 2.12   Guilds of London sample cards

icon language so dense that it inhibits play or makes it more intimidating to learn the game. You do not want "language independent" to mean "equally incomprehensible to everyone."

We will discuss more about localizing for different languages in Chapter 6.

ICON RESOURCES

There are many excellent resources for free icons for your game. While they are all fine to use in prototypes, please check the license agreement for each of these for whether they can be used in the final commercial product. Here are several top resources:

- **Game-icons.net** has over 3,500 black and white icons that are free to use. They are similar in style, searchable, and each can be set to specific color. They are also available in both SVG (vector) and PNG (bitmap) format. More about the difference between these formats was discussed in the Software Tools section of Chapter 1.

- **TheNounProject.com** has millions of icons. They can be freely downloaded for personal use (which includes prototypes), but if you wish to use them for commercial purposes you will need a paid account. Paid accounts also get access to the ability to colorize the icons and download them in more formats.

- **Open Icon Library** (https://sourceforge.net/projects/openiconlibrary/) includes thousands of icons. While designed for computer application toolbars and buttons, there are a wide variety of icons that can be used in games.

- **FlatIcon.com** has a vast array of full color icons. For a commercial product you will need to give attribution, but a membership allows for full use.

In addition, a simple Google search with the word "icon" will turn up useful results surprisingly often. For example, I was recently doing a political game and needed an icon that looked like the Capitol dome. I typed "capitol building icon" and was treated with images as in Figure 2.13.

At worst, if you find a photo that you want to turn into an icon but has too much detail, it is fairly easy to learn the skill of bringing a screenshot into Illustrator or Inkscape and tracing the outline. Even a poor artist like myself can do that. A search on *auto trace* will yield many tutorials on this topic.

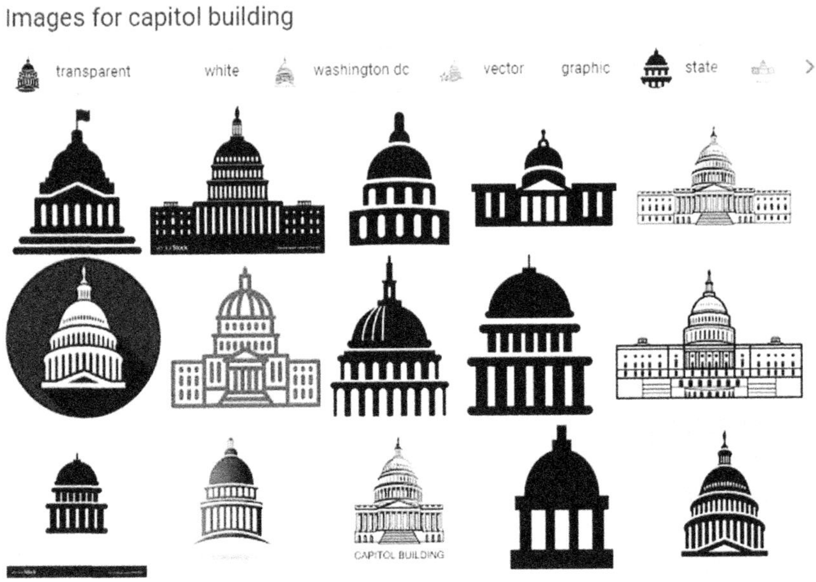

Images for capitol building

FIGURE 2.13   Google image search results for "Capitol Building"

FONTS

Fonts can quickly set a tone or evoke a theme. However, there are a few key rules for proper font usage in good graphic design.

Don't Use Too Many Fonts

While there are millions of free fonts available, avoid the temptation to use them all in your project. Most cards, rules, and other game elements will benefit from using at most two fonts: one for headers and one for text body.

For thematic reasons, it may make sense to use multiple decorative fonts for different factions to set them apart and make it easier for players to identify which components go with which factions. For example, my game The Ares Project features four very different factions. Each used a different decorative font for the card titles, but the main text always used the same font.

Don't Sacrifice Readability for Style

While evoking a theme is important with graphic design, it does not override usability. And for a font, the critical factor is how well it can be read.

It is important to go back to our discussion at the start of this chapter between artistic elements and gameplay elements. Feel free to use highly decorative fonts for the artistic elements. That's where you want to support the theme. However, the text that, for example, explains the special ability of a card needs to be clear and readable.

Another factor is font size. Experts recommend that the smallest font size used for cards is 6.5. But that size should only be used for clear, legible fonts. More decorative fonts should be larger. You should also consider how far players will be from the text. If something needs to be read from across the table, you may need 18 or 24 point. A good rule of thumb is "1 point per inch of viewing distance." So 6 point can be comfortably viewed from 6″. Obviously there are practical considerations, particularly at larger distances. But this is a good starting point.

Use Styles Consistently

There are several schools of thought about how to use bold, italic, and other text elements to draw attention. Some designers like to put all keywords in bold. Others like to capitalize them or put them in italics. Regardless of the stylistic choices you make, ensure that you are consistent. Once players get used to looking for keywords in a particular style, it will cause confusion if one card or game element omits it.

Use Font Sizes to Establish Importance

The size of fonts can be used to establish hierarchy. The eye is naturally drawn to large characters first and then will drill down to smaller items. Here again is the sample card from The Expanse (Figure 2.14).

Notice that the largest font is reserved for the Action Point value in the upper right. This is the key piece of information on the card. Then your eye is naturally drawn to the faction flags and event text, due to their size and high contrast background.

The title of the card, which is of lesser importance, is superimposed on the card artwork, which makes it blend a bit more into the card itself.

Finally, the other elements which are not as important, like the "AP" under the Action Point total, the card number, and the player count, are small and not distracting. The player count is only needed at the start of the game, and the location on the bottom of the card makes it easy to quickly ruffle through the cards and pull out the necessary ones.

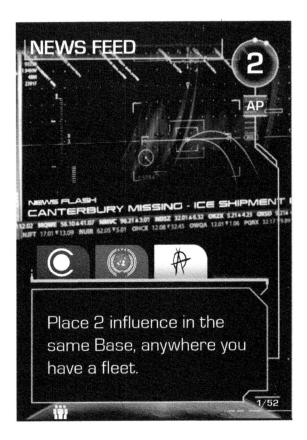

FIGURE 2.14   Production card from The Expanse

This echoes our discussion of the Three Reads that opened this chapter. Hierarchies are good.

Carefully Consider the Background

As alluded to above, the contrast between the text and the background is critical for making sure the text is easy to read. The simplest way for good contrast is to simply have black text on a white background, or vice versa. (Black text maybe slightly preferred for production considerations. More on that in Chapter 6.)

Avoid placing important game text on top of textured backgrounds or images. If necessary, carefully consider the contrast and look at each card to make sure that the text is clear. Sometimes it helps to outline black text on white or white text on black. Also, make sure to leave sufficient room around the text. Crowding the text will make it less legible.

Resources for Fonts

DaFont (dafont.com) and **Font Squirrel** (fontsquirrel.com) are both excellent resources for free fonts, although search by license to make sure you can use the font for your final intended purpose. If you are a subscriber to Adobe's Creative Cloud (see Chapter 1), you also have access to their extensive font library.

Creating an Icon Font

One thing that can be challenging is using special icons as part of your text. This can be a great technique for simplifying your text and making it consistent and understandable for the player (Figure 2.15).

One technique is to simply put spaces in your text, leaving blanks for the icons, and then later placing the icons over the text using your graphic program. While doable, this can make text modifications more challenging.

A better way to deal with this is to create an icon font. The websites **IcoMoon.io** (https://icomoon.io/) and **Fontello** (http://fontello.com/) both allow you to upload your own SVG files (easily exported from vector software like Illustrator and Inkscape) and create a custom icon font. Then, when using the font, you simply type the letter "A," for example, to place your mana icon in the text.

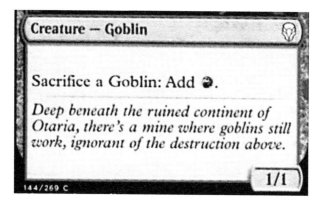

FIGURE 2.15   Inline icon on a Magic: The Gathering card

Now, when you need to edit the text, the icon flows with it. Much simpler!

If you are extensively using the icons at Game-icons.net, there is a specific font creator for that. It is located at https://github.com/toddfast/game-icons-net-font.

To make this technique even more powerful, graphic designer Daniel Solis has developed a technique that allows you to embed special codes in the data file for your mail merge, which result in them being automatically replaced with the icons on import. The following video link explains the technique for InDesign: www.youtube.com/watch?v=X5eTBrXRhyk

Component.Studio and nanDECK also includes tools that allow you to embed icons in text strings, either through alternate fonts or pointing to an image file.

Adding inline icons is an advanced technique, but one that is worth learning.

COLOR

Using color to indicate different game features, like which pieces belong to which players, is a common technique in graphic design for games. There are many, many resources about color theory and selecting color palettes, and so we will not delve into that here.

However, games do have requirements that go beyond that which is needed by making logos, for example. If color is going to be a functional part of the game, it is important to ensure that the colors chosen are easy to distinguish. Games have had unfortunate choices, like forcing players to distinguish between reddish-orange and orangish-red pieces. Make sure that your colors are easy to tell apart.

In the interest of accessibility, it is also important to take into consideration those that have various forms of color blindness. Color blindness affects 1 in 12 men and 1 in 200 women. As a designer, you want your game to be enjoyable and accessible to as many people as possible. Cutting out a significant portion of the population is a poor business strategy. Paying attention to this also has the happy side effect of making your colors easier for everyone to distinguish in dim light or glare.

There are two main techniques for dealing with color blindness that can be used separately or in conjunction. The first is selecting colors that can be distinguished by the color blind.

There are a variety of tools that can be used to see what your game materials will look like under several common forms of color blindness. There are different types of color blindness, so you want to make sure to check them all.

Color Oracle (colororacle.org) allows you to upload artwork and view them under different filters. **Toptal.com/designers/colorfilter** will display a web page with different colorblind conditions, and **Asada.website/cvsimulator/e** is similar, but designed to work on mobile devices.

If you're using Photoshop, you have access to a series of filters for testing color blindness. The webpage www.adobe.com/accessibility/products/photoshop.html gives full details about how to use this. Component.Studio, discussed in the previous chapter, also includes color-blind filters so you can see what your components will look like to people with different conditions (Figure 2.16).

In addition to color selection, the graphic design can use patterns, shapes, or other symbols to distinguish in addition to color. These can be subtle, so as not to detract from the overall aesthetic, while still giving a hint to players that have difficulty with colors.

A terrific example of this can be found in Ticket to Ride (Moon, 2004). The cards are distinguished by color, which is the first thing most players

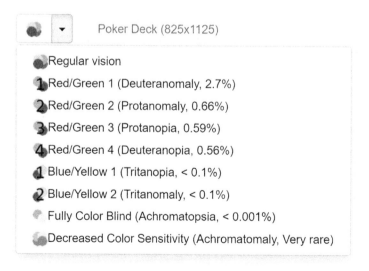

FIGURE 2.16   Component.Studio color blindness filter options

will notice. However, they also have different train car types and a different symbol in the corner so that players who have issues with the colors have something to fall back on. The symbol in the corner is a particularly nice touch, as players will be able to reference it when the cards are held in their hand and splayed (Figure 2.17).

DIVERSITY

When designing character art for your game, attention needs to be paid to the diversity of the characters. Players like to choose avatars that represent themselves or put themselves in the shoes of others.

The player base of board games has grown and diversified over the years. Where board game conventions in the 1970s and 1980s were the domain primarily of young white males, conventions now are family-oriented and have attendees of diverse races and genders. Reflecting that in your game is not just good business for you but also helps keep the overall game market growing. Appealing to as many customers as possible is always a positive step.

Diverse body types also have the happy side effect of making the characters easier to distinguish from a distance (Figure 2.18).

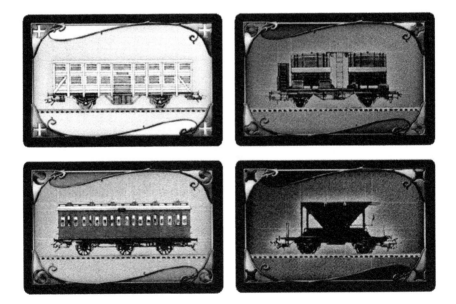

FIGURE 2.17   Ticket to Ride cards. Note different icon symbols in corners

FIGURE 2.18   Characters from The Dragon & Flagon

MENTAL MODELS

Recently I heard an interesting anecdote. A mother and daughter were on the bottom floor, standing in front of an elevator. The daughter said, "Shouldn't there be a Down button, so we can tell the elevator to come down to get us?"

Maybe she was asking this in earnest or maybe she was just joking. But this nicely illuminates the role that mental models play in our lives, especially around technology, where so much of what happens is hidden from our view.

The girl had a mental model that the buttons were sending a message to the elevator, not of where *she* wanted to go, but where the *elevator* should go. If you think about it, it is not a completely unreasonable thought. We often ask people to come pick us up and usually tell them how to get to where we are, not where we want to go.

This concept of mental models is critical to the way we think. Whenever we walk up to anything, whether it's a stovetop or a door or a game, we conjure up a mental model of what we need to do to achieve the effect that we want.

And designers have the opportunity – more correctly the responsibility – to build elements into the design that subtly guide the user into creating the correct mental model. As a simple example, let's talk about doors, especially in office buildings and hotel lobbies, where they try to make fancy glass doors that don't have knobs. The user decision to be made is – do I push or do I pull? And on what?

A properly designed door typically has features that clue you in as to what you should do. When you are supposed to push, many doors have a flat vertical plate that is on the side of the door where you should push. And if you are supposed to pull, there is a handle that by its shape and location says "pull me."

By far the best book I have ever read on this topic – and one of the best on any topic – is *The Design of Everyday Things*, by Don Norman (Basic Books, 1988).

Norman introduces standard terminology for these features, including the useful terms *affordances* and *signifiers*. Affordances are elements of your design that the user can use to actually do what they want to do. The pull handle on a door is an example of an affordance. Signifiers are features that are not functional but exist to give hints to the users about which affordances to use and how they operate. The push plate on a door is mostly a signifier, but also acts as an affordance, as it gives a better place to push the door rather than directly on the glass.

Norman identifies seven fundamental principles of design:

1. **Discoverability.** It is possible to determine what actions are possible.

2. **Feedback.** There is full and continuous information about the results of actions and the current state. After an action has been executed, it is easy to determine the new state.

3. **Conceptual model.** We already talked about this. The conceptual model enhances both discoverability and evaluation of results.

4. **Affordances.** Proper affordances exist to make the desired actions possible.

5. **Signifiers.** Effective use of signifiers ensures discoverability and that the feedback is well communicated and intelligible.

6. **Mappings.** The relationship between controls and their actions follows the principles of good mapping, enhanced as much as possible through spatial layout.

7. **Constraints.** Providing physical and logical constraints guides actions and eases interpretation.

The proper use of all these concepts is very important for the game designer to understand, internalize, and use in theme, mechanics, and graphic design. A game that has an easily understood conceptual model, and effectively uses affordances and signifiers, is a game that is going to be easy to learn and allow the players to focus on the action and not the rules.

Using Affordances and Signifiers

To illustrate affordances and signifiers a little bit deeper, let's talk about the humble scoring track.

As discussed above, mental models are the concepts that we have in our brain about how we expect something to work. If there's a difference between what we think is going to happen when we turn a dial and what actually happens, we get confused or make mistakes.

With all due respect to the Arabic and Hebrew readers of this book, most of the world reads from left to right or top to bottom. So when we see objects in a row we assume that it should be looked at going from left to right. This extends to quantities and time as well. If asked to order number cards or dates, the low numbers and early events go on the left and get larger as you move to the right. Left is the past, right is the future. This is culturally wired into our brains from a very young age, and it is a poor designer that goes against this trend. Similarly, people move clockwise around a ring.

So when you make a scoring track, scores should increase as you go from left to right or as you move clockwise. Unfortunately there is a commonly used type of scoring track that violates this principle – snake tracks. I hate snake tracks, especially those with no clear indication other than the numbers which way you should be moving. For example, I really enjoy playing Imperial Settlers from Portal. But the scoring track is horribly designed from a user-interface standpoint. You have to really focus when moving score markers. The numbers are not clear, it's arranged in a grid, and it's just a real pain. That arrows between rows needed to be included is a tacit admission by the graphic designer that the players will need help. And that's because it goes against our mental models (Figure 2.19).

I know it's not a scoring track, but a game that falls down on this is Chutes and Ladders. The board for this is a 10 × 10 grid of squares. At the

FIGURE 2.19   Snake Track

end of each row there's a tiny arrow showing that you should move up to the next row and start going the other way. If you're not paying attention to the numbers, it's very easy to move the wrong way when your turn comes around (Figure 2.20).

There is an extremely easy fix to these snake tracks. Don't make the rows parallel. If each row was angled upward at a slight angle, so it looks like a switchback or a Donkey Kong level, then two other mental models will kick in – following the path and moving upward is better than moving down. An example of what this could look like is shown in Figure 2.21.

Now let's look at affordances. Affordances are the actual things that we grab or manipulate to operate something, like a dial or button, or a game piece or a card.

The affordance on a score track is the piece that you move. This piece needs to do a few things. It needs to show clearly which space it is in. If it is along with other scoring markers, you need to be able to see them all, and it should be difficult to shift accidentally. Unfortunately, I've seen a number of games that break these rules. The biggest offender is the tall skinny cylinder as a scoring piece. This is a bad thing, as they easily get bumped and roll away, and the players lose track of the space it was in, and possibly the piece itself. Cardboard chits are much better as they can't be bumped. However, chits make it impossible to see pieces that are stacked beneath them. Personally, I like wooden discs the best. You can clearly see what pieces are stacked underneath them, yet they are not that easy to move.

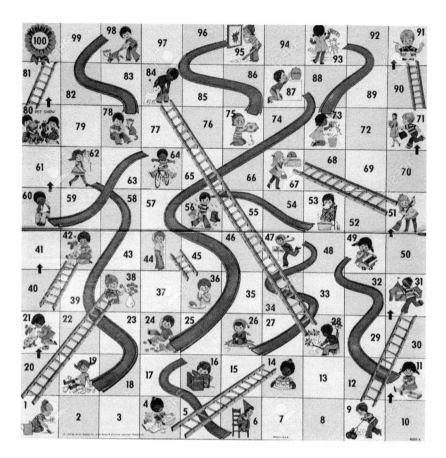

FIGURE 2.20 Board from Chutes and Ladders

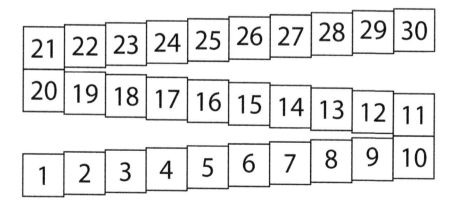

FIGURE 2.21 Example of an exaggerated angled score track

Signifiers are the ways that objects give us hints about how to use the affordances and what they do. For scoring tracks, these are the spaces and, particularly, the numbers in them. To be good signifiers these should have easy to read numbers, along with highlighted squares every five or ten to make it easier for people to calculate. Finally, if your track wraps around, make sure it's clear where the zero point is and wrap it in a "normal" fashion so it's easy for people to see how far ahead or behind they are.

Let's pull all this together in an example. Let's say that you have a game where only one person can be in a scoring space. If someone else is supposed to move to that space, they get bumped ahead instead. How can you use affordances and signifiers to make it easy for players to remember this? Here's one idea – make the scoring tokens fill up the space completely and give them domed tops so that they can't be stacked. Now the players are physically unable to put more than one scoring marker in a space, making it much less likely that they'll forget that rule.

As a designer, thinking about mental models, affordances, and signifiers can make your game a complete package that is easy to learn and play.

CARD LAYOUTS

Many of the graphic design principles we've discussed apply to card layouts. However, there are some considerations specific to cards.

If the cards are held in hand, keep in mind that most people splay cards to reveal the upper left corner. Therefore, your most critical information should be contained there. A traditional deck of playing cards has the number and suit in the upper left, for example.

Another thing to keep in mind is that you need a 3 mm safe zone around the edge of the card. Any card elements that are in this area may be lost due to misaligned trimming during the manufacturing process. We go into great detail about safety zones in Chapter 6 but keep that in mind when adding iconography.

Cards are also an excellent place to practice the Three Reads process of varying sizes and colors so that the players can focus on the correct information. For example, Figure 2.22 shows a card from Twilight Struggle. The first read information here is the icon in the upper left with the number (the red star) and the card title and artwork (*Fidel*). The icon is the most important information on the card. It shows which side is eligible to use the card Event (the lower paragraph) and the number of Action Points the player gets if the Event is not used.

FIDEL*

Remove all US Influence in Cuba.
USSR gains sufficient Influence in
Cuba for Control.

Remove from play if used as an event.

FIGURE 2.22 Fidel card from Twilight Struggle

For example, the Fidel Event can only be used by the USSR player (red star). If not used for the Event, the player gets two Action Points. That's very important information when you fan your hand of cards. The cards with higher numbers and your player icon will be the most important assets you have that round.

At first it seems odd that the card title and artwork are also part of the first read. These do not assist the players to play the game. They are, however, very important for thematic reasons. The prominence of the card title and art helps engage the player and transport them into the shoes of the leaders and frames the historicity of the game. This card is very successful at capturing the nature of Fidel Castro's revolution in Cuba and the impact that had on the Cold War. Also note that the title is upper case, whereas the explanatory text is standard upper/lower case, which also draws attention to this area.

The second read on this card is the Event text and the special *Remove from play* text, which is printed in red text. The latter is a smaller font size, but the red color brings it to the fore. The asterisk after FIDEL is a cue that the card is removed from play after the Event is used, and those two features working together make it unlikely that players will forget to remove the card.

The third read elements are the card number on top (the "8") and the EARLY WAR indicator. The latter is only required during setup, and the card number is only needed as a reference if you think you're missing a card. While the size of the EARLY WAR text is actually larger than the event text, it blends into the background as a result of being white text on a medium blue background.

As a counter example, take a look at the card in Figure 2.23. The artwork on this card is undeniably gorgeous, and the cards as a whole are very pleasant to look at. However, there are a number of graphic issues.

The first read on this card is the artwork itself. It so dominates the card as to make the other elements difficult to distinguish. And while it helps establish a thematic air, it does not impact or aid game play at all.

The second read is the suit and the star value, in the two upper corners. Finally, the third read is just to the left of the star value, and it describes what you need to do to collect the star value. This text is actually the key

FIGURE 2.23 Example card where art has trumped graphic design

part of the game, and yet due to placement, size, and font, it does not leap out at the player and is difficult to read once you do notice it. The decorative font does not help the player here. In addition, although hard to see in this image, there is a bevel effect on the font which further reduces the legibility.

USABILITY CASE STUDY: ECLIPSE

The 1975 game Stellar Conquest (Howard Thompson, Metagaming) is little known but incredibly influential. Its ambitious design had players begin at separate planets in their own corner of the board. They explored local star systems, colonized them, researched technology, and ultimately battled the other players for domination of local cluster.

It established the genre now called "4X" – Explore, Expand, Exploit, and Exterminate. It also demanded a lot from its players, as it was not a simple game. Players literally had to track their population and industrial output on a ledger page by hand. Population growth rates varied by planet habitability, and each planet produced ships based on its own industrial output.

Much of the game was spent with players having their heads buried in the colony production sheets, calculating compound interest.

And yet there was something incredibly compelling about the subject and scope. It was a natural fit for a computer game, where the machine could keep track of the math and allow the player to focus on the fun. Reach for the Stars (SSG, Keating and Trout, 1983) was an early contender. Master of Orion (Microprose, 1993) was another popular entry into this genre, and it continues today, with 2016's Stellaris, from Paradox.

However, the genre continued to be a niche product in the board game world. Perhaps the most popular implementation was Twilight Imperium (Petersen, 1997), which launched the board game company Fantasy Flight Games. While Twilight Imperium is still popular today, and is on its fourth major release, it is a big commitment to play. The game typically takes eight hours and is not for casual play.

In 2011, the tabletop game Eclipse (Tahkokallio, 2011) was released. It redefined the 4X genre for tabletop game, by creating the full epic experience in a two-hour package. And it did it, to a large extent, through superb use of graphic design. The remainder of this chapter analyzes the techniques that Eclipse used to create affordances and signifiers that streamlined play.

As mentioned earlier, one of the difficult and time-consuming aspects of Stellar Conquest was the bookkeeping – keeping track of production, the maintenance of your empire, population, and more. Shortening and streamlining that process is one of the core innovations in Eclipse.

In Eclipse, each star system is represented by a hexagon. A sample is shown in Figure 2.24. When a player takes control of a hex, they place one of their discs in the center. Most hexes have squares representing the production potential. When a player develops a hex they own, they place a matching cube on the space.

Each player has their own mat, where the cubes and discs are placed at game start. They are removed from right to left, revealing a number underneath. This number represents production of that particular type (minerals – brown, money – orange, research – pink). The discs have a negative number under them which is how much upkeep needs to be paid for the empire in money. Money is always orange, so the color here is a mnemonic.

So as cubes and discs are removed from the player mat and placed onto conquered systems, the additional production can just be read out. And as the empire gets larger, the upkeep will also increase. But there's no counting and adding up of different systems during the production and upkeep steps, like there is in Stellar Conquest. You simply read off the exposed

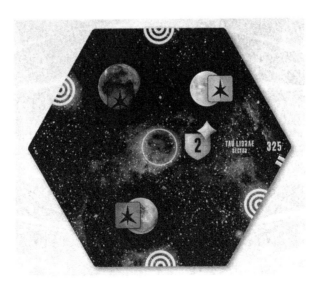

FIGURE 2.24 Hexagon map tile from Eclipse

numbers. And if you lose systems, you return the cubes and discs onto your player mat and the revised values are readily apparent. Eliminating the bookkeeping aspects saved hours of time over the course of the game (Figure 2.25).

One of the questions designers are often asked is whether they design "mechanics first" or "theme first." When asked this question about Eclipse, game designer Touko Tahkokallio revealed that this graphic design idea was actually his inspiration. The idea of removing cubes to reveal the current production levels was at the heart of the entire process. Graphic designer Sampo Sikiö was involved from the very early stages of the design. The focus on graphic design was literally baked into the design from the start.

Eclipse also masterfully uses shapes to guide players about what can and should be placed where. In the tile shown in Figure 2.24, cubes go on the squares and the ownership disc goes on the circle. However, another sample tile is shown in Figure 2.26. Notice that extra shape in the center? What could that be?

Well, it's the piece shown in Figure 2.27, which is called a Discovery token. If you explore a tile that has that symbol, you first place the Discover token, which must be dealt with before a player can claim the tile. These

FIGURE 2.25 Eclipse player mat with cubes and discs. The resource income is the largest uncovered value on each track

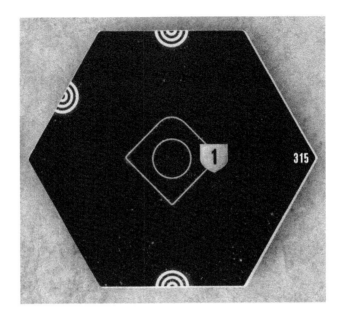

FIGURE 2.26   Eclipse map hex with spot for Discovery token

FIGURE 2.27   Discovery token. Note how shape matches with Figure 2.26

symbols being placed in the center of the tile do double duty. First, the peculiar shape indicates that something is supposed to go there, with a matching shape. If it was just a larger circle or something like that it would not draw as much attention as this shape.

Also, placing the Discover tile covers the circle where you place the ownership token. This serves as a subtle rules reminder to the players that the Discover tile must be removed before the ownership disc can be placed.

A similar shape technique is used for Diplomacy and Victory tiles. Players take the shield-shaped Victory tiles when they win a battle and can trade Diplomacy tokens with other players to score points. As is common in Eclipse, the shapes are distinctive.

There is a limit to the number and type of these tokens that players can accumulate. Figure 2.28 shows the part of the player mat where it is stored. The rule is that you can have up to four Diplomacy and Victory tokens in total and up to three of them may be Victory tokens.

This is the type of rule that can be easily forgotten by the player, resulting in lots of rules lookups, a reference card, or simply mistakes in play. However, the graphic design of these spaces is a great example of "mistake proofing." It is clear which tiles can go where, and that a space can only take one tile. The rules are cleanly built directly into the graphic design.

The second edition of Eclipse, Eclipse: Second Dawn for the Galaxy, released in 2020, still found some areas to improve in the graphic design. For the new version, the large player mats were split into two pieces – a mat for tech and ship designs and a vacuum-formed container for tracking resources. The latter also doubles as storage for the faction's components. The ship layouts now include a silhouette of the miniature, to make it that much simpler for new players to identify which goes with each. Many other small tweaks improve the "quality of life" for the player through graphic design. For example, the use of icons was made more consistent, with less reliance on color. Figure 2.29 shows an image of the new hex tile. You can see how icons are now included in the production squares, which circumvents color blindness issues.

There are many other examples of smart choices in Eclipse, including consistent iconography, use of color, and more. If you're interested in exploring this topic more deeply, studying Eclipse is a terrific method. It's also a fun game to play, so there's an added bonus.

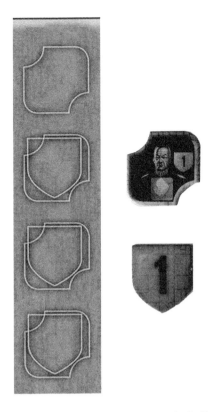

FIGURE 2.28 Eclipse Diplomacy and Victory track (left) and corresponding tokens (right)

FIGURE 2.29 Eclipse second edition map tile

CHAPTER 3

Writing Rules

THERE IS PROBABLY A board game convention somewhere every weekend. And while I obviously can't go to all of them, I do attend my fair share, which means a lot of quality time on airplanes.

As part of my travel preparations, I always bring along a few rulebooks, both printed and PDF. I bring the rules for games I consider purchasing, looking at the latest to learn about new mechanisms, and even go over the rules for older games I own to rediscover some classics.

Yes, I admit it – I enjoy reading rules.

However, I am by far the outlier. Most people hate reading rules. And yet games must come with rules of some sort. A game is defined by rules.

Video games have mastered the art of tutorial. When computer games first came out, they were accompanied by thick manuals, just like board games. But over the years, they have dispensed with the manuals. Computer games are designed to teach you the game as you play – either with introductory tutorials that show you the core mechanisms or by gradually introducing new concepts as you progress.

Board games do not have this luxury. You will need to teach the rules to the players, and almost always this will take the form of a rulebook. Learning the rules is a huge barrier for entry to most players. It is critical that your rules effectively engage and teach players. This is the first impression many will have of your game, and care should be taken in their construction and presentation.

This chapter discusses the key issues to consider while writing rules.

WHEN TO WRITE THE RULES

A perennial debate among game designers is when to write the rules. Some designers, myself included, prefer to write rules earlier in the process and keep them updated as they evolve. Others feel that, since the rules are changing frequently, it is a waste of time to keep an up-to-date rules document.

Both viewpoints are valid, and what you do will depend on your process. The reasons for waiting until the end of the design to write rules are obvious, but the rationale for constantly revising rules takes a bit of explanation. It seems, at first glance, to go against the advice of iterating as quickly as possible. Why take time to write rules?

To be clear, I don't advocate writing rules from absolutely the first moment. At that stage you should just be pushing pieces around or scribbling on cards and brainstorming different ideas. The velocity of change should be high, and you don't want to impede that by worrying about writing things down. However, once things settle down a bit, writing down the rules has a variety of benefits.

First, it gives you a record of previous versions. Often, when you run into a roadblock, it can be useful to look at earlier iterations of the rules to seek inspiration or see if the germs of a new direction can be found there.

Also, the act of writing rules down can be very helpful for realizing where issues and loopholes may be. More importantly, having to clearly express a rule in written form is a great way to judge its complexity. Often rules that seem simple in your head, and when pushing pieces around, become complex when written.

A good guideline is that a rule that is hard to express succinctly is a bad rule and should be replaced or eliminated if possible.

Finally, if you are working on multiple projects, or if you sometimes need to take a break from a design to help overcome a design block, or because of life reasons, it can be incredibly helpful to have a set of rules that you can refer to when you pick the project back up again. It is surprising how sometimes the small details of how a game works get forgotten or changed in between design and test sessions. Having a written record of the rules can jump-start your design process.

The rules you write during development don't need to be organized, have diagrams and examples, or even be complete. You don't need to update your rules every time you make a design change in a session. They need to work for your purposes and accomplish the goals while putting forth a minimum amount of effort.

But if you prefer to just wait until the very end of your process to write rules, you'll be in good company.

THE PURPOSE OF RULES

If you haven't written rules before, you're going to find that it's harder than it looks. When sitting down to write my first ruleset, I was woefully naive. I had written computer code for decades prior, and the tasks seemed similar – take a complex problem, break it down step-by-step, and write down the instructions. And I did that, and the rules were horrible.

Before we get into why, let's take a look at an example rule, from the game Advanced Squad Leader (ASL) (Greenwood, 1985):

> **11.6 CC vs an AFV:** In order for a MMC to advance into a Location containing a manned unconcealed enemy AFV, it must first pass a PAATC (failure of which causes the unit to become pinned). SMC, Fanatic, and Berserk units are exempt from PAATC. A leader may use his leadership modifier to aid any units in the same Location with their respective PAATC even if he does not advance into the Location himself. All Inexperienced Infantry must take a 1TC rather than a NTC in order to advance into a manned enemy AFV during the CCPh, no further PAATC is necessary in order to attack it during CC. A unit which passes a PAATC must immediately advance into the AFV Location; it may not await the outcome of another unit's PAATC before deciding whether or not it wishes to advance. PAATC attempts need not be predesignated.

Most people think this is a terrible rule. It reads like gibberish, and most likely you have no idea what this is about. However, for those who play Advanced Squad Leader, it is very well written. It is precise and covers several different exceptions to the core rule in a succinct way. If you're interested, by the way, this rule is about Armored Fighting Vehicles (AFV's – or "tanks" to you and I), and what happens when a squad of soldiers (Multi-Man Counter or MMC) moves into their space.

This rule is great as a reference for experienced players, but terrible at explaining what is happening to the new player.

And this is what I had missed in my first attempt at rules writing. Rules serve two main functions: *Tutorial* and *Reference*. "Tutorial" means teaching and explaining the game and getting the players to understand how to play properly. The key word here is "teach." "Teaching" implies that it is not just a step-by-step guide. It is giving someone a framework to understand why they're doing what they're doing and to put it in a context to make it easy to remember.

The second function of rules is to act as a reference guide, so that people who go back to the game after a long absence or who need to look up a detail during the game can easily find the information they are looking for and get back up to speed. It is frustrating for players to have a question and not quickly resolve it, or for a play session to be messed up because a rule was forgotten or overlooked.

I have coined the terms *Rules as Tutorial* and *Rules as Reference* for these two approaches.

My "computer program" style of rules at best were Rules as Reference, a dumping ground for all the rules. But it did not provide an on-ramp for players to understand the overall structure of the game. It just assumed they would read through all the rules and go through the procedures step-by-step and be fine. It made it more difficult than needed for new players, and the ratings and sales of the game suffered.

People did not enjoy flow charts as much as I thought.

There are several techniques that have been developed over the years to allow rules to be both a teaching guide and a reference. While we will go over several of these, the general principle is to start at a high level, giving players an overview of what they are trying to do, and then gradually drill down into the details. The high-level picture gives players a map in which they can fill in the details as they arise.

For example, you should explain as early as possible what players need to do to win the game. Do not simply leave it until the end, even though that is a natural progression, as victory is usually the last part of a game. Your rules should not be a "whodunnit," where you hide the surprise in the final act. By understanding what they need to do to win, players can give context to the other rules and systems and how they fit into that. It is not just a series of disconnected mechanics that they need to remember. It is a series of steps required to win, which is much easier to internalize.

If the way to win is to accumulate the most "honor," then as the players read the rules and see that something gives them "honor," they realize that it is very important and can place it properly in their mental map. It gives them a guidepost to work with when learning the game. If they don't know that having the most honor wins the game, then it just becomes another resource, and everything can get muddled.

BASIC RULES SECTIONS

Here is a recommended outline for rules. Most follow some form of this, so keeping this will help people who play lots of games get oriented. Not all of these sections will be required in all games, particularly for simpler ones. However, this is a good starting point. The key takeaway here is that you want to start at the high level and then drill down and get more detailed as you progress through the rules.

- Overview/Fluff
- Objective
- Contents
- Setup
- General Flow of Play
- Details
- End of Game
- Index

Overview/Fluff

Begin with the overall scope of the game and what players are trying to do. You should let the players know a little bit about the world and who they represent. This is the opportunity to get the reader hooked and excited about playing, in the same way that the opening line of a book should be memorable and grab the reader's attention. Here is the opening from my game Space Cadets: Dice Duel:

> Space Cadets: Dice Duel pits two starships against each other in quick-paced combat. The players are divided into two teams, each team playing the crew of their ship. The team will win or lose together. The game ends when one side destroys their opponent by

causing four points of damage through torpedoes or mines. Each ship has six stations. Engineering generates power for the other stations. Helm maneuvers the ship on the map. Weapons loads the torpedo tubes to attack the enemy. Sensors locks onto the enemy so torpedoes can hit, and uses jammers to stop the enemy from locking on. Shields helps protect the ship from enemy torpedoes. Finally, Tractor Beams can grab the powerful crystals, move the enemy ship on the map, and launch Mines. There are no turns in Space Cadets: Dice Duel. The game continues with players acting as quickly as possible until one side wins. Each player will be in charge of one or more of these stations, or have the overall role of Captain to coordinate everything.

This gives an overview of all the different player roles, and a little bit about why they are important. Now when reading the details of the different stations on the ship, you have some idea of how it all fits together.

Objective

Tell the players what they need to do to win the game. This helps orient the players when reading the rest of the rules and lets them know what to focus on. Here is that section from Dice Duel:

To win the game you must cause four damage to the enemy ship, destroying it. Damage is caused by torpedoes and mines. The Weapons and Tractor Beam rules give all the details.

You'll note that this information was actually included in the introduction. However it is worth repeating here because if the players are using the Rules as Reference – perhaps just skimming through after having not played for a year – they will not think to read the introduction to learn how to win. It's clearly spelled out in the Objective section.

Also, I included the detail that damage is caused by torpedoes and mines. This wasn't strictly necessary here. Later in the rules on torpedoes and mines it says they cause damage. However, now, right from the start, the reader knows that torpedoes and mines need to be used to win the game. So that gives another signpost for players to slot later information into their mental map.

Finally, since this is the first time in the rules proper that the terms "torpedo" and "mine" are introduced, and I don't explain how they work or how damage is caused, I provide a reference where those details are contained. This both informs the player using the rules for reference on where to go for that information and also assures the new reader that they haven't missed something.

Contents

This section details all the game components. If space permits, including pictures of each component type is a big plus. You should also include quantities of components so that players can make sure they have not lost any pieces.

Setup

Detail how to set up the game. For complex setups, it can be very helpful to have a full diagram showing what the table will look like after setup is completed. A narrative description is often included with numbers referencing the different setup steps in the diagram. Figure 3.1 shows an example setup diagram from the game The Networks (Hova, 2016).

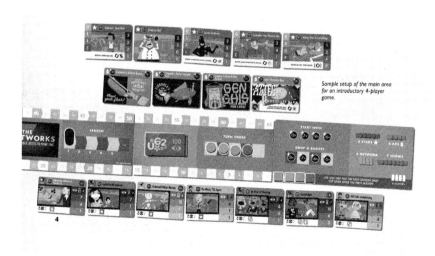

FIGURE 3.1   Setup diagram for The Networks

General Flow of Play

This section gives a brief overview of the overall structure of the game. For example, it is played over three rounds, and each player takes turns within a round until all players pass.

Don't go into deep detail in this section. Only provide enough information so that the overall structure is understandable. Again, you are trying to orient the player so that they have a 30,000-foot view of the general flow.

Details

This section contains the bulk of the rules, as you now drill down into the details. There are a variety of ways to structure this depending on how your game is organized.

One option is to simply give more details of each of the steps of a turn and what happens in each. Another is to first explain common mechanisms (like conflict resolution) and then go through the turn sequence. Each game will have its own requirements.

Make sure to include examples of play. A narrative explanation of how rules are applied can go a long way to clarify the meaning of rules. However, do not only have a rule in an example of play. Examples should only show rules that are elsewhere included in the rules. Players will not think to look in examples to find actual rules.

End of Game

This section has the details of how the game ends and how victory is determined. The objective should be explained at the beginning of the rules and how the game ends should be in the General Flow of Play. But this section can recapitulate and expand on those as needed. Most players will flip to the end of the rules to see information about the game end, so putting this information at the end, even though potentially redundant, will be helpful.

Index

Depending on the complexity and length of the rules an index may be helpful. This is strictly in the Rules as Reference category. It can be a boon to players who need to look up a specific rule or concept.

GAME-SPECIFIC TERMINOLOGY

Many games will have special terms that they use. Sometimes these may be a regular word used in a specific way. For example, you may earn "Honor" by completing missions, and this may be used to determine victory. Other times your words may be made up for the game. Your magical force may be called *Aetherium*. Regardless, there are a few guidelines for how to treat these **Game Terms** in rules.

The first time you use a Game Term in your rules you should make sure that it is explained at that point. For example, in the previous paragraph, the idea of the Game Term was introduced, so that you naturally understood what I meant when I used it. In addition, it is recommended to capitalize Game Terms, and bold them the first time they are mentioned, as was also done in the last paragraph. This helps by both drawing the reader's attention to the fact that this is something that has special meaning in the game and informing that they should not just treat it as a normal word.

It also acts as a reference for people checking the rules later. If players need to scan the rules to find out what a Game Term means, they can simply look for the bold instance.

Ideally the rules for that Game Term are right there, but sometimes it is not possible to do that while still preserving the flow of the rules. In this case, you can either give a quick explanation of the meaning, include a cross-reference like "see page 5 for details," or simply say something like "more on this later."

Another option is that if you have a lot of specific terminologies, you can include a Glossary at the start of the rules. A sample Glossary for Imperial Struggle (Gupta, Mathtews, 2020) is shown in Figure 3.2.

Earlier in this chapter I showed a rules excerpt from my game Space Cadets: Dice Duel. If you go back and look you'll notice that I did not capitalize or bold the Game Terms "torpedo" and "mine." This was one of my earlier games, before I realized the importance of this. If I were redoing this game today I would absolutely have capitalized those Game Terms.

Some games, in the interest of world building, will create their own terminology for common things. Dice, Turn, Card, Health, and even Mana are all common terms that will make your rules much easier to understand. Be very wary of using your own invented terms for these. You may think it's cool to call dice Crystals and rolling them Scrying and turns

List of Game Terms

- **Action Points** (abbreviated as **AP**) are what players spend to perform actions during Action Rounds in *Imperial Struggle*. There are three types of Action Points, each of which can be spent on a different set of actions:
  - ◊ **Economic Action Points** (**Ⓔ**). See 5.4 for the ways players can spend Ⓔ.
  - ◊ **Diplomatic Action Points** (**🖋**) See 5.5 for the ways players can spend 🖋.
  - ◊ **Military Action Points** (**Ө**) See 5.6 for the ways players can spend Ө.
- **Bonus Conditions** on Event Cards indicate how, when playing an Event card, a player can gain the card's **Bonus Effect**. See 5.2 for more about Event cards.
- **Britain** is often abbreviated as **BR** in cards and rules.
- **Connected:** Two spaces are connected if they have a thin black line linking them on the map.
- **Conquest Points** (CP) are earned by winning certain theaters of war. They are spent to acquire eligible Territories from the opposing player. See 7.2.1 for how to spend Conquest Points.
- **Debt**, like Treaty Points, is used as "wild" AP. Many Event cards inflict negative effects on the player with the worse Debt situation. The "D" symbol refers to Debt; if it is accompanied by a British pound symbol, it refers to British Debt, or if accompanied by a French livre symbol, it refers to French Debt. See 6.0 for more details about Debt.

 This British War tile forces the French to take 1 Debt, as indicated by the livre symbol alongside the D for Debt.

- **France** is often abbreviated as **FR** in cards and rules.
- Keywords are present on most Ministry cards. They have no inherent function, but many Bonus Conditions reference keywords, and they grant strength in some Theaters as well.
- **Major Actions** and **Minor Actions** are the two action kinds in *Imperial Struggle*. They always have a type (Economic, Diplomatic, or Military) and grant AP that match their type. Minor Actions have more constraints on how their AP may be spent. See 5.3.2 for more on Major and Minor Actions.
- A **Theater** is a component of a War. To resolve Wars, players resolve each Theater in turn, determining a winner and awarding **Spoils of War**. Each Theater has its own **Bonus Strength** list, which shows the players what assets, alliances, and keywords will contribute to their strength in that Theater (7.1.3, 7.2).
- **Treaty Points** (TRP) represent the countless bargains, arrangements, and concessions that emerge from statecraft, warfare, and diplomacy. In *Imperial Struggle* they are used as "wild" AP. See 9.0 for specifics and restrictions on the use of Treaty Points.

FIGURE 3.2 Imperial Struggle Glossary. Note that this ruleset uses the Outline Case structure, allowing for easy cross-reference to the relevant rules

Cycles and say fun things like "At the start of the cycle scry your crystals," but I guarantee you that the players are just going to teach it as "at the start of your turn roll the dice."

Remember: the rules are an obstacle for your players to get through, to be able to enjoy the experience of actually playing the game. Don't make it harder for them.

If you are making a game based on a license, then it may make sense to use terminology from the universe to bring your game into that world. In that case, it is more reasonable to assume that players are bringing preexisting knowledge to the game. Even so it is important to make sure everything is explained in a way that players who are unfamiliar with the property will still find the game accessible.

Consistent terminology is another important facet of writing effective rules. While a specific Game Term will naturally be used the same way throughout the rules, you should also make sure that everyday words are used as consistently as possible. For example, let's look at my game Super Skill Pinball. This is a "roll and write" game simulating, not surprisingly, pinball. Each player has a laminated sheet with boxes on the bumpers, targets, flippers, and other pinball features, with different die faces inside them. You roll the dice and move your ball token to a box with a matching die face to your roll and cross it off. If you can't mark off a space you lose the ball.

The first time I wrote the rules I used a variety of terms for these different elements. Sometimes they were "boxes," other times "spaces" or "features" or "areas." Sometimes I said you "marked off" a box or "crossed it off" or "filled it in" or "completed it."

Yes, people were mostly able to figure out that these meant the same thing. But there's no reason for me, as the rules writer, to make them jump through an extra cognitive hoop. I did a special editing pass (several, actually) to make sure that the same terminology was used. Everything was called a "box," and you always "mark" it.

When learning to write in school, we were all taught to vary our sentence structure and word choice so it would feel fresh and lively. In school we used a thesaurus to try to find alternate ways of saying something so that we didn't use the same word repeatedly. In rules writing you need to go against that training. The same action should always be called the same thing. Mixing it up is not helpful in this situation.

STRUCTURAL LAYOUTS OF RULES

Over the years, several different techniques have been developed to design rulebooks that both teach and serve as a reference. In this section we discuss several of them. Keep in mind that there are always different ways to approach this issue, and the requirements of a long, complex game will be quite different than a game with a single page of rules. However, these are all good techniques to consider as you compose your rules.

Separate Rulebooks

A very direct approach to Rules as Tutorial versus Rules as Reference is to simply have two separate rulebooks – one a teaching guide and one a reference. This technique was used to a limited extent with the first release of The Settlers of Catan in 1995, which included the core rules in one book and then a separate Almanac booklet which gave full details on all the game elements. Fantasy Flight Games has standardized on this technique for their more complex games, always including a Learn to Play Guide and a Rules Reference Guide (Figure 3.3).

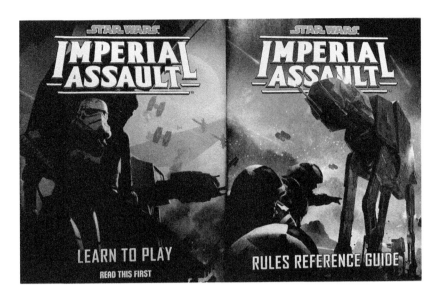

FIGURE 3.3 *Imperial Assault* (Kemppainen, Konieczka, Ying, 2014) includes a Tutorial rulebook and a Reference rulebook

A Learn to Play Guide can be structured in a variety of ways, including a tutorial or a play which introduces concepts in a controlled sequential way and leaves details and exceptions for the Rules Reference. It can also be much more conversational in tone and approachable for the player. Another positive is that it can help the players teaching the rules by giving them an outline of how to explain the game.

GMT Games produces sophisticated conflict simulation games. They take a similar but distinct approach to this, with most of their products including a Rulebook and a Play Book. The Play Book includes detailed examples of the play, sometimes playing through an entire game, and also designer notes, explanatory text, and other supplemental information. The rulebook contains the precise game rules, with index. The difference with the Fantasy Flight approach is that with GMT the player is expected to have at least a passing familiarity with the rules to fully understand the Play Book, whereas the Fantasy Flight Games Learn To Play Guides assume no knowledge. While Fantasy Flight has an edge in approachability, the GMT Play Book examples help resolve rules confusion.

The disadvantage of the two-book approach is that it adds additional cost to the game, both development and production costs, and it is asking more of the player by having them read two separate documents to fully learn the game. For these reasons, this technique is typically limited to more expensive and complex games.

Reference Column

In this technique, each page of the rules is divided into two columns. The main rules column is about two-third of the page width. The smaller column contains highlights, summaries, or supplemental information about the main rules.

An example of this can be seen in Dominion (Vaccarino, 2008) (Figure 3.4). The primary rules are on the outside part of the page and the

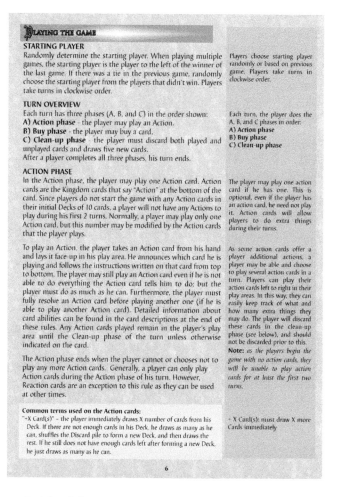

FIGURE 3.4   Rulebook for Dominion, showing sidebar layout

supplemental information near the spine. Placing information here has several positive aspects:

- Summarizing the core rule in the main rules provides a hint to the reader that this is the key point.

- Summarizing also provides an easy reminder to the returning player of the key information, like setup and turn sequence.

Pulling examples and supplemental information out of the core rules makes reading them easier and less choppy.

Outline Case Format

Originally pioneered in wargames of the 1970s, Case format uses an outline-based system to number each rule. This is typically used when many cross-references are required. For example, the Advanced Squad Leader rules are done in this format. The starting number in the example (11.6) means that it is the sixth rule in section 11. If any future rule needs to refer to this, it can simply say "see 11.6" instead of "see the rules on how MMCs attack an AFV on page XX."

The downside, of course, is that it makes the rules look more intimidating than perhaps they are. Readers first seeing an Outline Case format sometimes think they might need to memorize the rule numbers, which is, of course, not required. For this reason, this style is typically only seen in more complex games that have a lot of cross-references.

Card Almanac

In this style, the core rules of the game are up front in the rulebook, and then rules for specific cards or special powers are placed at the end, in a reference guide. This is a way of giving the high-level view first and then diving down into the details when the player has more information about the full structure of the game, or, more frequently, only as it is needed. The games La Granja (Keller, 2014) and my own The Dragon & Flagon use this approach.

Distributed Rules

Related to the Almanac style, some games spread the rules out over the components, typically cards, reserving only the base, core rules to a rulebook. Dominion (Vaccarino, 2008) and Magic: The Gathering are classic examples of this format, with the latter having rules for thousands of cards on the cards themselves. This gives an easy on-ramp for players, as they only need to learn the basics and can learn about the cards gradually as they play. While this system has many positives, there are also drawbacks:

- Players can spend a lot of time trying to understand their cards, particularly at the start of the game.

- For complex cards, the text may get small, which can make it difficult and intimidating for some players to read.

If there are questions about the rules on a card, and hands are hidden (as most are in games of this sort), there can be no way to resolve the question without revealing information. Card Almanacs solve this by having a separate booklet with more details, but often this is impractical in a game like Magic.

Programmed Instruction

For a complex game, sometimes it can be useful to introduce the rules gradually, through a series of games. This is referred to as Programmed Instruction. It was first used in the game Starship Troopers (Reed, 1976), where a series of seven missions brought the players up to speed on the complete rule set.

Sometimes it is not a series of missions, but different versions of the game. Through The Ages (Chvatil, 2006) starts the players with the Basic Game rules, then has rules for Advanced and Full games. The Full game includes all the rules and is the way that the game is intended to be played.

While Programmed Instruction can be effective at gracefully introducing players to the most complex version of a game, there are pitfalls that have caused it to fall out of favor. The most glaring is that, while this is an effective Rules as Tutorial, it does a very poor job of serving as Rules as Reference. If you need to look up a rule, you need to know which version of the game it is included in, and often find yourself flipping between many different scenarios to find where a specific rule is explained.

In later printings of Through the Ages, the Basic/Advanced/Full rules were supplemented with a separate booklet which was just the full rules presented as a normal rulebook. The game Squad Leader (Hill, 1977) used a Programmed Instruction approach. However, after several expansions, the rules were so spread out over different modules that the entire series had to be scrapped and re-released as Advanced Squad Leader (Greenwood, 1985), which eliminated the Programmed Instruction approach and replaced all the separate rules books with a single loose leaf binder.

Ironically, the single rulebook for ASL was so intimidating that to give an entry point to new players, the ASL Starter Kit #1 was released in 2004, which used a Programmed Instruction method and a series of scenarios to gradually introduce the rules. However, this time there was ultimately a single definitive rules source. This underscores the necessity for both Rules as Tutorial and Rules as Reference.

While full-blown Programmed Instruction is rarely used today, its shadow does remain in the form of Beginner or Expert rules, which some games include. For example, an expert game may include variable player powers.

This is best used if the additions do not add much rulebook overhead, by being contained on cards, for example, or if the additional rules are easily contained in a block at the end of the rules, and do not significantly add to or modify the earlier rules. For example, say you are designing a battle game with infantry, tanks, and planes. The planes add a lot of complexity, so you want to put them into an expert game. This is a good application of Expert rules, as the rules for planes can be segregated and grouped together.

However, let's say that for the expert game you want to augment the types of actions the tanks can take. Now your rules for tanks are split between two parts of the rules, and the rules are less useful as a reference.

Some games have interspersed different versions of the rules as they would normally occur, but show them in a different color or background so that the reader knows they only apply to a particular level of game. Generally, this is not well-received, unless used sparingly. It interrupts the flow of the reader, and most will end up at least skimming those portions to see what they are missing.

The best example of introducing new rules into the middle of existing rules can be seen in Risk: Legacy (Daviau, Dupuis, 2011), which introduces new rules on stickers and has blank areas in the rules where these are placed when introduced into the game. That way when needing to use the rules for reference, the rules are where you expect them to be.

INTERACTIVE AND VIDEO TUTORIALS

An increasingly common aid to learning games is a video tutorial. There are services that can make these for you (like Watch It Played), or you can try to make one yourself. Videos have proven to be a very effective teaching guide and can make it less intimidating for your players to get started.

Another option is the *integrated tutorial*. With this method the components come prepackaged in a specific order so that players can go through a few preprogrammed turns and be taught the game. This was used to great effect in Fog of Love (Jaskov, 2017), which gives the players the rules as part of the deck, as they play through the first game. They literally do not have to open the rules at all in order to begin playing.

This cannot be done for all games, but there are elements that can be included, like giving extensive examples of how to play in the rules, preferably using the cards in the order they come in the deck, or, if you have a deck construction game, having "starter decks" included that can get the players moving quickly. Whatever you can do to get the players past the rules hurdle will be a plus.

Be aware though, that if you want a specific card order in your prepackaged decks, it may cost additional money for the manufacturer to set up a system to ensure that it is done correctly.

YOU AND THEY

Where possible, use second-person phrasing. "You draw a card" is preferable to "The player draws a card." It is more succinct, but also more engaging for the reader, as it is active and dynamic. This extends to activities as well. The headings for the setup instructions for Pax Pamir (Wehrle, 2019) are:

- Build the Draw Deck

- Create the Market

- Take Player Pieces

The rules writer could have said *Building the Draw Deck,* but the active form is more engaging.

Third person is sometimes unavoidable for clarity or phrasing. However, when using third person, the singular "they" should be used. For example:

If you play a red token, select another player. They draw a card and place it into their hand.

They reads clearly here and is inclusive. Alternatives like *The player draws a card and places into his or her hand* are clunky and difficult to parse. I have also seen rules that alternate between using masculine and feminine but find this can trip up readers. It is much simpler to just use singular They.

If using clearly gendered names in examples, then gendered pronouns can be used. For example:

Susan draws a card and places it in her hand.

RULES EDITORS

Rules editors are invaluable. Most likely you will have spent way too much time editing, tweaking, and changing your rules, and you just stop seeing them after a while.

If you are signing your game with a publisher, they will provide rules editing services. However, if you are self-publishing, you should invest in a professional rules editor. They will bring a fresh set of eyes to your rules and quickly be able to tell what is confusing. A good rules editor will also be able to suggest structural changes so that the rules flow better and identify where examples might be needed.

Depending on the level of edit you are looking for, the rules editor can even completely restructure the rules to fit into one of the structures discussed in Chapter 3. This will depend on how comfortable you are with your ability to write and structure rules.

Note that rules editing is different from rules layout. A rules editor is looking at the text of the rules to determine what is clear, what edge cases need to be explained, and similar items. Rules layout is the physical act of doing the rules layout in a program like InDesign, with page textures, header styles, example graphics, and more. Typically, these are two different people. The rules layout person assumes that your rules are in a finished state and simply lays in the text. They may find an obvious spelling mistake, but that's about it.

While you should have a rules editor reviewing the near-final rules, most of the editing work will fall on you. Make sure to check for:

- Consistent terminology (word usage, spelling, and capitalization)

- Component counts (number of tokens, cards, etc.)

- Examples of play (play them through with physical components)

- Edge cases (what if there's a tie, or you can't draw from a pile?)

Personally, I like to print out the rules when doing this final edit. For some reason I find it easier to spot issues on the printed page than on the computer screen.

My first published game, The Ares Project, was about building up armies and battling your opponent. There were detailed rules about exactly how to conduct a combat. However, it wasn't until after the game was released that I realized, after fielding questions from players, that the rules never explicitly say who wins a battle. It does say that if the battle goes for six rounds without a player being eliminated, the defender wins. And it did say that the battle ends when one side is eliminated. However, it didn't say what that meant. Most players picked up the obvious meaning that the side that is eliminated loses, but the rules did not actually say that. And it didn't say what happened if both sides were eliminated on the same round.

This is a classic example of the one rules issue that is notoriously hard to find: *The rule that isn't there.* You know the rules. And you can read a rule and realize if it doesn't make sense or is just wrong. However, if a rule is missing, it's really hard to spot. You know the rules, so your head just papers over it.

The best way to catch these types of issues is through Blind Playtesting. We're not going to talk about playtesting techniques in this book, but since this one is so bound up in verifying that your rules are good, let's take a moment.

Blind Playtesting means that you give your game to a group to play, but you don't teach them, and you don't answer questions. They learn it on their own, and then play it while you watch. This is invaluable for seeing what rules they missed, what they misinterpreted, and what is causing confusion.

However, it is really hard to do Blind Playtesting for a number of reasons. First, it can take a while for people to read the rules during the session, so you may have to send someone the game first and have them learn it, then arrange for the face-to-face session. Second, and more importantly, it can be tough for designers to be in the room and not help players. And it can be tough for players to have the designer sitting there in the room but have to muddle through the rules to figure something out.

Ideally your players would be able to play in an interrogation room, with you sitting behind a one-way mirror watching them. But I'm guessing you don't have access to that.

An alternative that is becoming more common is remote recording. One of the players sets up a tripod or a mount for their phone or tablet and records the entire play session. The video is then sent to the designer for review.

It can be a real eye-opener for designers to watch people play their game without their influence. Some concepts that you thought were simple will end up tripping people up, and you will even see people playing large sections of the game incorrectly.

If you have the opportunity, doing this sort of remote Blind Playtest will go a long way toward vetting out any lingering confusion and issues with your rules.

II

The Development Lifecycle

CHAPTER 4

Alpha Prototypes

THIS BOOK IS NOT about how to or where to get ideas, it is not about playtesting, and it is not about how to polish your design. It is about the physical prototyping and production of games.

However, I would like to frame this chapter with a strong recommendation – spend as little time as necessary on your prototypes, particularly in the early stages of design. There are two reasons for this. First, you want to be pushing pieces around as quickly as possible. Spending time theorizing and designing a game in your head is valuable, but you'll find out pretty quickly what is working and what isn't when it actually gets tried out.

The second reason is that your game will be terrible. The mechanisms won't work. Choices will be obvious. It will be too long, too slow, or too boring.

This is not an indictment of you as a designer. All designs are terrible when they first get played.

And so, you will need to throw away large parts of your prototype. This means that you're also throwing away the time you spent to construct that prototype.

Most of this chapter will describe techniques for getting a prototype to the table quickly. These are all suggestions, not hard-and-fast rules. Everyone has their own process, and because game design is inherently a creative endeavor, you need to find one that inspires and motivates you.

For example, I know a successful game designer and publisher who is an artist. And one of the first things he does is draw the cover art for the game. This is antithetical to everything I am describing here. However, for him, it helps to organize his thoughts and gives him a reference point, a vision statement for the game, in a sense.

Your personal process may also change over time, so don't be afraid to let that happen. As I've gained more experience with Adobe Illustrator, I've gotten very quick at creating bare-bones cards, and it's now often faster and simpler for me to do that than use index cards. However, sometimes the physical act of writing on a card acts as a catalyst for brainstorming and creative thought, so I do still fall back on that.

The point is that hopefully the ideas in this book will give you some place to start. But if something else works for you, that's great. But understanding what is required, what publishers are looking for, etc. will allow you to make the best use of your time and rapidly iterate. The key goal of this phase is to be able to try, discard, and iterate as quickly as possible.

CREATING CARDS

Index Cards

Index cards are a fantastic place to start for alpha cards. The 3″ × 5″ cards give plenty of space to write, and they can be rapidly modified. Having multiple colors of index cards also makes it easy to make multiple types of cards for your test if that is required.

Index cards are also very easy to modify during a playtest. Keep a pen or marker handy, and don't be afraid to modify values on the fly if something isn't working. Similarly, you don't have to design everything at the start before you begin testing. It's perfectly fine to leave blanks or just put "special bonus" or something similarly generic. When you get to the point of actually using that bonus, make up something that seems right and write it on the card.

In his book *Boardgames That Tell Stories* (Portal Games, 2014), designer Ignacy Trzewiczek describes how the game 51st State literally began as a stack of blank index cards. He knew the world he wanted, sat with a friend, and dealt out blank cards to each. They imagined what they wanted to do within the world and made up cards to do it. Gradually the game took shape, and 51st State and its successor Imperial Settlers both became very successful publications – with not a blank card in sight.

While for most purposes, 3″ × 5″ index cards work fine; some players find them unwieldy if you have many of them in a hand. If necessary, you can cut them in half, into a 2.5″ × 3″ card, which is very close to a standard Poker-sized card (2.5″ × 3.5″). You can also cut 4″ × 6″ cards in half for a slightly oversized Poker-sized card (3″ × 4″).

Printing onto Cardstock

If you create the cards on a computer, you can print onto either paper or cardstock. Paper is best when used in conjunction with sleeves. If you want to just use the cards "as is," you should print onto cardstock.

If you are using general drawing software like Illustrator or Inkscape, it is a good idea to create or download standard card size templates to work from. If you are creating your own template, make sure that you leave room on the edges for the printer margin. Home printers cannot print all the way to the edge of the page.

Also, the cards should be butting up against each other. Do not leave "gutter" space between the cards. You may need this if you do a production card sheet, but for early prototypes, it will be much easier to cut out the cards with a rotary trimmer or blade if the cards are right up against each other.

Figure 4.1 shows my standard card template for 2.5″ × 3.5″ cards.

You should learn and use layers in your graphics software of choice. Think of layers as a transparent sheet that you draw on and can turn on and off at will. You can also lock layers so that geometry on them can't be selected or change the order of layers to bring certain features to the fore. For example, the card outlines and background graphics should be on their own layer in your drawing, so you can lock them and not accidentally select the geometry when drawing on top of them. If you have multiple sheets of cards, you can put each onto a page in a separate layer rather than to create a series of sheets. This can reduce the effort involved in changing background images since they are shared between multiple cards.

If you are doing double-sided cards and your printer can do double-sided printing, make sure the two sides are on different pages and not just different layers on the same page. Also make sure that your templates are centered on the page both vertically and horizontally, so the faces match up.

If your printer doesn't do double side and you need to flip it over and run it through again, then you can just keep the opposite side on a separate layer and turn it on or off as needed.

Another protip for double-sided cards: Only put the card outlines on one side of the card – preferably the front face. The back of the card should not have any lines between the cards. See Figure 4.2 for how this looks.

The reason to do this is because printers, even ones that can print double side, are not great at lining up front and back (called "registration").

FIGURE 4.1   Card template

There will be some offset, particularly if you have to feed sheets twice and flip them over. If there are lines on both sides you can guarantee that when you cut on the lines on one side they will be mismatched on the other. If you don't have lines on that back your eye won't notice the mismatch nearly as much. Your content on the back will still be off-center, but it will take a more sustained look to realize it.

When this sheet is cut, the slices are lined up to the borders on the faces. So those which are the most noticeable if they are off, and most important functionally, will be accurate.

Paper and Sleeves

An alternative to index cards is to use card sleeves to hold slips of paper. For this method you will need a supply of "penny sleeves." The term "penny sleeve" comes from the cost, which is usually a few pennies each. But it is highly dependent on the quantity you purchase.

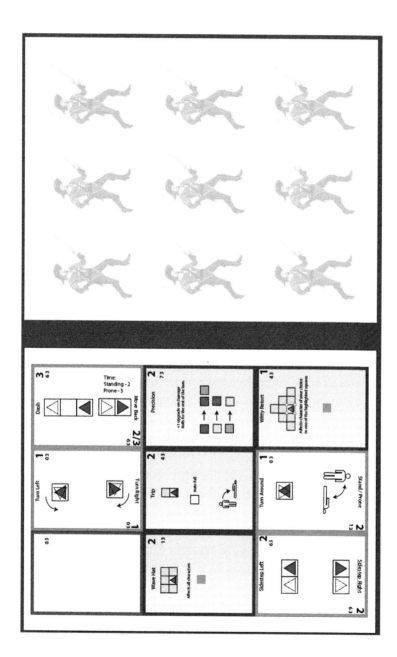

FIGURE 4.2 Double-sided cards. Note that the lines for cutting are only on one side

In this technique you typically use a sheet of regular copy paper and a rotary cutter to slice it into appropriately sized slips. You can hand-write onto these after cutting them or use a computer to print on them in advance and cut on the lines.

When inserted into the sleeves they can be "backed" on "unbacked." "Backing" means sliding another card into the sleeve behind the paper, to give it more rigidity and make it feel more like a traditional playing card. You can use any card for this. One source is simply the card decks you have lying around the house. Another is finding a source for surplus or little-used cards from trading card games like Magic: The Gathering. Most game stores that deal in Magic will sell generic "land" cards very inexpensively or even give them away.

Typically backing is used to help make the cards easier to shuffle and not as easy to crease. If you're doing lots of shuffling and similar card handling, index cards can be difficult to work with and can easily be bent.

In alpha, early alpha, in particular, this may not be an issue, but it can be if a particular prototype is seeing a lot of play.

There are, of course, downsides to early sleeving. First, it is a lot more work to create the deck than just writing on index cards. Second, it is much more difficult to change and iterate on during and after a play-test. With index cards, you can just write on them. With a sleeved card, you need to fish out the insert, modify it, and then put it back into the sleeve.

If you need to have multiple different card backs, you have a few options, depending on whether the card backs are showing important game infor-mation or not, like a reduced strength ability on the flip side.

If it's just different card types, so the backs of each deck are the same, you can get sleeves that are not transparent on both sides but have one side that is opaque. These are available in a wide variety of colors and patterns. You can also use different backing cards to differentiate the decks. For example, you can use Magic cards for one deck and a traditional playing card deck for another.

If the backside of the card is important to see, and you still want to use sleeves, you have two basic options. First, you can insert slips of paper both in front of and behind your backing card. Or you can also use card-stock instead of paper and write or print on both sides and skip using a backing card.

Dry Erase Cards

A specialty option is Dry Erase Cards. These are blank cards which can be written on with dry erase markers and wiped clean. These can be fantastic for brainstorming and prototyping, as you can rapidly update the cards and not have all the cross-outs that you get with index card prototypes.

However, be careful when you need to shuffle or mix up the cards as the markings are very prone to get smudged and become hard to read. But for the right application (cards that are placed up on the table, for example), this can be a nice option.

TOKENS AND TILES

For alpha prototype tokens and tiles I simply draw onto index cards and cut them out or print them onto cardstock and slice them out. Remember, if you have small tokens, it may be faster to cut off strips of them from your sheet and then simply use scissors to cut them off rather than a rotary or box cutter.

Where possible, avoid non-square tokens at this stage. In Chapter 2 I extolled the virtues of using different shapes as a graphic design tool to help players. This is not the time to introduce that. Squares and rectangles are going to be a lot faster to prototype.

If you must have circles, either invest in a circle punch or simply cut off the corners of the square tokens to make octagons, which are a close enough approximation for circles at this stage.

Backing onto Chipboard

To give your tokens or tiles more heft and durability, you can back them onto chipboard. The simplest way to do this is to print the tokens onto full-sheet labels and then stick them onto a same-sized sheet of chipboard. While not something I would do for first prototypes, if you have a lot of tokens and are worried about a stray cough or sneeze sending everything flying, this method allows you to make tokens and tiles that will stand up to repeated play.

As discussed in Chapter 1, there are various weights of chipboard. For this purpose, I recommend using at least 30-point chipboard to get a decent feel.

There is a specific technique that is good for transferring a full-page label to chipboard and keeping it aligned. Peel away the backing from a short edge. Leave the rest of the backing on. Align the edge with the chipboard

FIGURE 4.3   Transferring a label to chipboard

carefully, starting with one corner and working your way across. Then gradually peel away more of the backing and press the label flat as you go. Peel and press, peel and press as you work your way down the length of the chipboard.

Do not completely remove the backing before you begin to stick it down to the chipboard. This makes the label very difficult to work with and opens you up for alignment issues, creases, and bubbles. Just gradually peel off small sections and stick them, and you'll get a nice even bond.

Figure 4.3 shows this process.

Once the label is fully applied, cut the tokens or tiles out as normal.

As an alternative to a label you can use a spray mount. However, there are some caveats with this process, described in detail in Chapter 1. To summarize, pay careful attention to ventilation and use cardstock instead of paper to make it easier to peel off and reposition if necessary, before fully adhering the sheet.

GAME BOARDS

Boards are typically larger than the letter or A4 paper that can normally be printed at home. If you need to print out a board, you have two main options – assembling multiple sheets or using an outside printing service.

Assembling

As a first pass, using 8.5″ × 11″ sheets of cardstock is a great solution. You can lay them out on a table and draw on them. A few pieces of tape will secure them to the table if necessary – painter tape is great for this as it is easy to remove from the paper without damaging it.

If you have created your board in a graphics program, you will need to print it out in separate sections. One option to do this is using the website rasterbator.net. This site allows you to upload an image (JPG, PNG, or GIF), and it will spread it across multiple pages and allow you to download a multi-page PDF. Although free, the site owner does request donations if you are using the service to help cover expenses (Figure 4.4).

Windows Paint, to the surprise of many, can also print image files across multiple pages. To get to this option, go into the "page setup" menu. You will see the Scaling option in the lower right and can fit it to a grid of pages. This program is included in all Windows installations (Figure 4.5).

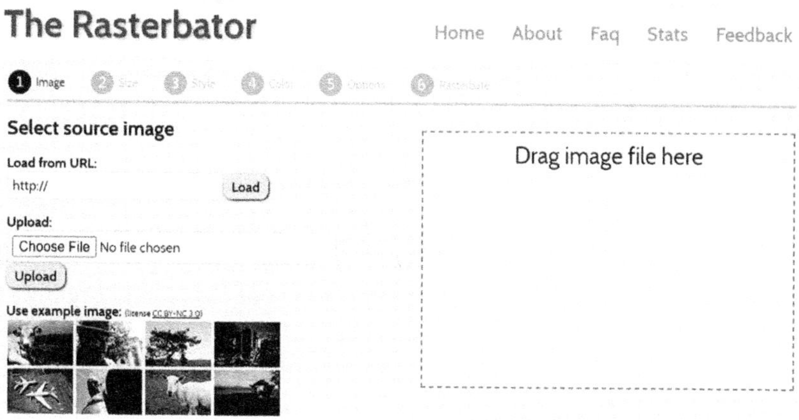

FIGURE 4.4   Rasterbator

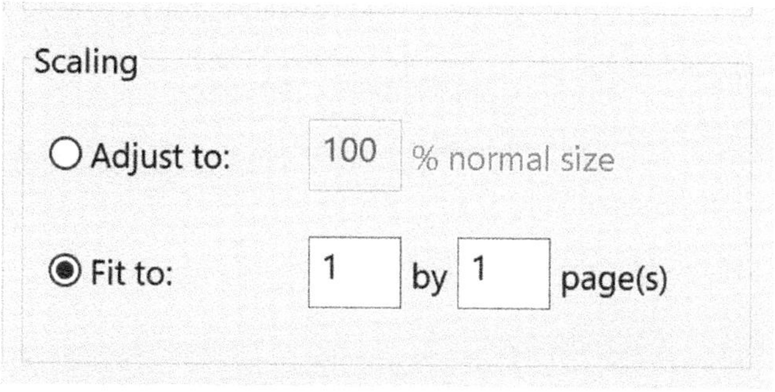

FIGURE 4.5   Windows Paint options

Adobe Acrobat can also spread a large PDF over multiple pages. When you print a PDF file from Acrobat, you can select the Poster option, which will give you the options shown in Figure 4.6. This allows you to spread the image over multiple pages, and Acrobat will handle the overlap, taking into consideration the printer margins.

If you use a Mac, the program SplitPrint, at $6.00, is an inexpensive way to print across multiple pages (www.splitprint.com).

If you are printing onto multiple letter-sized sheets, you have the option of printing onto label stock and then adhering that to the chipboard. This is a costly and labor-intensive process and is probably best used for later beta prototypes. If you do make this type of mounted board, you probably won't want to tape it to the table for fear of damaging the board. Instead you can tape them from behind to make folding hinges or keep the board in separate sections and use small binder clips to hold them together.

Printing Service

Most office supply stores (like Staples) offer printing services, as well as stand-alone shops like FedEx Office. These will print a 22″ × 17″ poster for about $15. You can also get lamination and mounting services for an additional cost, but those upgrades are best saved for beta testing.

It is best to use the thinnest material on offer. This will not only save money but will also make it much less likely to hold a curl, making it simpler to tape to the table. Thicker materials will have a nasty tendency to pop up off the table if you store them in a tube (which is the best method).

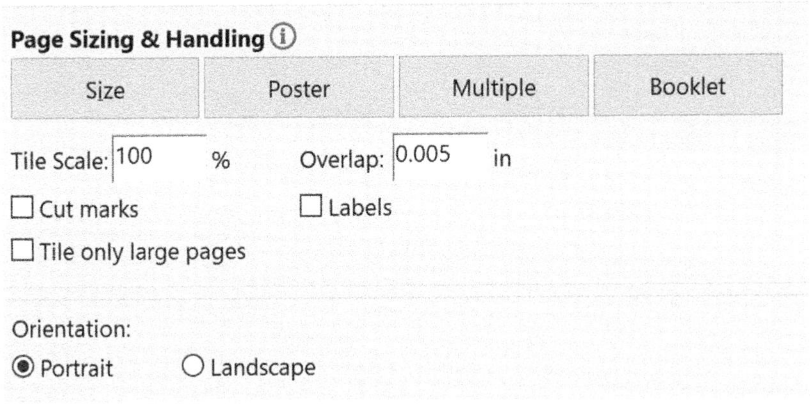

FIGURE 4.6 Adobe Acrobat Poster option

Acrylic Sheet

An alternative to taping your board onto the table is to invest in an acrylic sheet. Wargamers have used this method for decades to make a secure playing surface for paper maps. If you are unable to find an acrylic sheet at your local craft or hardware store, you can instead purchase an inexpensive poster frame and use the plastic insert to lay over your board.

HEXAGONAL TILES

It can be tricky to prototype hexagonal tiles, but here are a few tricks.

First, the super simple method. And if you can use this, this book just paid for itself.

Index cards can double as a hex grid. If you lay them out in a brick pattern, each card is adjacent to six other cards. This is 100% mathematically equivalent to a hex grid and is way, way simpler to construct. (Figure 4.7).

FIGURE 4.7   Brick pattern

This method is even used in published games, like Undaunted: Normandy (Benjamin and Thompson, 2019).

This doesn't work if the tiles can be rotated during play, but otherwise it is equivalent. In fact, there are several games that have shipped with "brick pattern" boards, where the spaces are rectangular. Many players perceive them as being friendlier and more approachable than hex grids.

If you do need to rotate your tiles or do want to have true hexagons for aesthetic or other reasons, one option is to simply use the token techniques described above, either printing them onto cardstock or onto a label and sticking it to chipboard. Cutting hexagons out can be laborious, as you can't use a rotary cutter and must do the cuts by hand. One way to make it slightly faster is to do all the cuts in one direction, sliding your straight edge across the page without rotating it. You can do all the cuts with three passes at different angles.

The last option I will present is purchasing blank hexagonal tiles. These are available at Game Crafter, Print Play Productions, and Spielmaterial in a variety of sizes. You can then print on sticker paper and apply those to the hexes.

You won't want to cut out the stickers into hexagons – at that point you might as well just do a full-page label and cut the chipboard. Instead you can cut the label sheet into squares and stick those into the center of each hexagon. Alternately you can purchase label paper with circular labels of an appropriate size and print onto those. A circular label in a hexagon, appropriately sized, will leave a very little area around the edges of the hex.

CUSTOM DICE

For early designs, I highly recommend simply using a standard die with a reference card showing what the different numbers mean. This will make it much simpler for you to iterate over early prototypes, as only the reference cards need to be changed. The dice can just be grabbed from your standard prototype kit.

For example, my game Space Cadets: Dice Duel is a real-time speed game, where each player has a station on a starship like shields, sensors, or engineering. They roll specialized dice for their station and have to match symbols to power them up.

I knew from the start of the design that it would require custom dice. But for most of the development I simply used normal D6's and gave the players a station mat that showed the meaning of the symbols. Figure 4.8 shows examples of the Sensors and Weapons stations for normal D6's.

Speed is important in Dice Duel. There are no turns, and players roll the dice as quickly as possible to get the sequences they want. Even so, the extra cognitive load on the playtesters to learn the charts was worth it in terms of time saving for development.

Once the game stabilized, I moved to the next stage, which was stickering the dice. Formally, this should be considered a beta technique and included in the next chapter, but it is included here to keep the dice discussions in one place. Again, I would like to stress that you should use normal dice for as long as possible.

The simplest way to create stickers for dice is to print them onto a full-page label sheet. The sheet for Dice Duel is shown in Figure 4.9. Note how the distribution of face matches the normal pip versions in Figure 4.8. You will also notice that I included stickers for blank faces. This is a personal

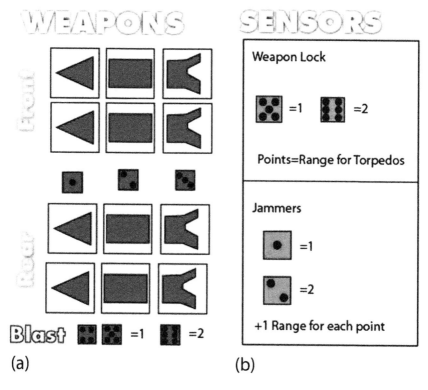

(a)   (b)

FIGURE 4.8   Weapon and Sensor stations with dice pips

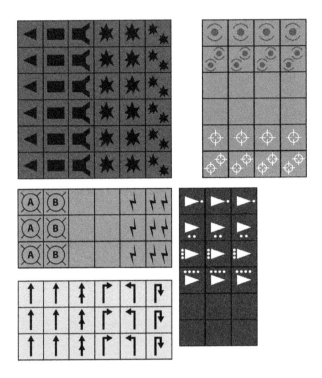

FIGURE 4.9   Sticker layout for Dice Duel dice

preference, but I find that having all sides stickered makes the dice feel better when rolling and also in general gives a more finished look.

When cutting these out it can be best to use a box cutter and straight edge rather than a rotary cutter or scissors. You want to slice through the label, but not the backing. If you simply cut the individual squares all the way through, you will find that it can be difficult to remove the backing. Plus having 114 little squares isn't the easiest thing to work with.

By applying medium amount of pressure and cutting the label but not the backing, you will find it much simpler to flex the page and to peel off the sticker. It is also much less likely that the stickers will get lost.

As mentioned in Chapter 1, there are two basic types of blank dice – standard and indented. Indented are slightly more expensive, but the wear on the stickers will be greatly reduced (Figure 4.10).

FIGURE 4.10   Stickers on indented versus normal blank dice

MINIATURES AND STANDEES

In early prototypes, instead of using miniatures you can substitute stand-ees. This is a piece of cardstock that has a picture of the character on it and stands vertically on the board.

The standee itself is best formed as a folded piece of cardstock. That gives them strength and stiffness and also makes it easier for them to stand up straight and not lean over. The best way to lay these out in your graphics package is to do a single side and then duplicate the other side through rotation or reflection.

Figure 4.11 shows the prototype standees for The Dragon & Flagon. In this case, facing is important – the players need to know which direction the character is facing. To indicate this, we added a grey screen to one half showing the rear. Other techniques can be used, but if you do need to indi-cate the front, make sure that there is some distinguishing characteristic.

Once these are printed, first create a score line down the hinge for all the standees before cutting them out of the sheet. You create a score by lightly dragging a blade along the line, guided by your straight edge, with-out actually cutting the cardstock. This will create a nice, even fold.

After you create your score, then cut out the standees using your tech-nique of choice.

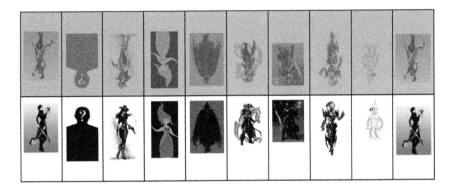

FIGURE 4.11   Sheet of standees

FIGURE 4.12   Binder clips on standees

For bases, while it is possible to purchase the plastic standee bases that you find in games, they tend to be costly in small quantities when other options are available. I recommend using binder clips, which are readily available in office supply stores. In addition, they can be purchased in a variety of colors and sizes, making them very versatile.

Figure 4.12 shows a medium binder clip being used to hold a standee. If desired, the wire forms can be removed with pliers after the standee is inserted. If you choose to do this, wear protective eye equipment in case the wire shoots out of the binder clip.

An alternative to standees is to use miniatures. At this stage, you will not make custom miniatures, so they can either be borrowed from other games or purchased specifically for your prototype. The latter can be expensive, so it is best used for beta prototypes, if at all.

I keep an eye out for opportunities to purchase miniatures in bulk. Ebay, game store flea markets, and cons can yield great deals on large supplies of miniatures. Reaper also has annual Bones Miniatures collections on Kickstarter, which gives a huge variety of miniatures to have available for prototypes.

CHAPTER 5

Beta Prototypes

THERE IS NO CLEAR line between alpha and beta prototypes. It is simply a useful shorthand to indicate a design that it is going through rapid iteration versus one that is more mature. It is also not a one-way trip. Many designs move to a beta prototype, but then run into a sticking point that requires rapid iteration over alternative mechanisms. For these, it is more productive to stick with alpha prototyping methods.

REASONS FOR BETA

To reiterate, the purpose of the alpha/beta distinction is to invest as little time as possible into something that may change, for two purposes. First, time is a valuable resource, and your project will get finished faster by spending time appropriately. Second, the more time you have invested in a component or a mechanism the harder it is going to be to let it go. Keeping time invested in an element to a minimum will help you make better design decisions.

There are several reasons you may want to move to a beta prototype.

Enhance Thematic Immersion

Some games stand squarely on the shoulders of their mechanisms. Lost Cities (Knizia, 1999) could have any number of themes and be just as delightful. However, for some games, engaging the players with the theme is important to the desired experience. Sometimes, with barebones components it can be difficult to judge whether the final thematic artwork will elevate gameplay.

As an example, my game The Dragon & Flagon was about fantasy tavern brawls. It had tables that the players could stand on and mugs they could throw. The Dragon & Flagon was inspired by an earlier game, Swashbuckler (O'Neill & Taylor, 1980), that simply had table and mug tokens that sat flat on the board. We wanted to up the ante with three-dimensional tables the players could stand on and wooden cylinders for mugs. Testing those components was valuable, both to see if players reacted to them in a positive way and to make sure that it was physically easy to move the standees around, place them on tables, etc.

Demonstrations for Publishers

When you are pitching to publishers, you may want to increase the quality of your prototype. Most publishers take many pitches and are good at seeing the core of your game and are not unduly influenced by graphics. However, they are human and first impressions matter. I asked several publishers about this, and this is a typical response:

When Taking a Pitch, How Much Does the
Polish of the Components Impact You?
Not exceedingly, but it certainly doesn't hurt. The game needs to be clear and understandable when looking at it, so any components that have complex use should be made nicely, etc. Sometimes when a prototype is too fancily printed I get a bit concerned like they're more into splash than substance. And of course it depends on the game. If the table presence is a big selling point we need to understand how.

As a reminder, the term "table presence" means a game that draws you in just by looking at it. This can be done with three-dimensional structures, miniatures, or terrain, for example. Having "table presence" was one of the design goals for The Dragon & Flagon, so we needed to up the prototype quality for our beta. Figure 5.1 shows the final production, to give an example of what we had in mind.

Marketing Demos

If you are self-publishing your game, giving demos at conventions and through videos can be an important element of your marketing plan. In this case you will want to make prototypes that look as close as possible to your vision of the final product. Unlike publishers, an average con-goer is not as used to looking past basic graphics. Playing what feels like a finished

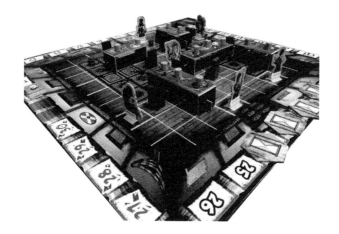

FIGURE 5.1   Final production of The Dragon & Flagon, showing "table presence" of three-dimensional components

product will make them more likely to take your game seriously, be interested in sitting down to play, or add their name to your mailing list.

Final Artwork and Component Testing

When the final graphic design and artwork is complete, it is highly recommended to create a single set that is as close as possible to a mockup of the final production. This will help to ensure that all components are present, that the colors of different components work well together, and that all components fit into the proper spaces and reveal any final usability issues. If you license your game to a publisher, it is still important as the designer to take this step if possible, particularly if the publisher has not. Unfortunately, when at this final stage, people are often in a rush to get the files to the printer and don't want to take this final step. This can leave you open to undetected issues, however.

If you have the means and time, this final beta can also be used for *blind playtesting*, which is discussed in Chapter 3.

UPPING THE GRAPHIC DESIGN

When you move into beta, you want to really focus on the graphic design, particularly usability. Remember the comment from the publisher earlier in this chapter: The game needs to be clear and understandable. Early in a playtest you need to focus on getting the mechanisms to work together and produce the experience you want, so you can wave away some of the issues with graphic design. That's not the main focus early on.

However, at this stage, you need to start upping the ante on graphic design, focusing on iconography, signifiers, and accessibility. As an example, here is a progression of cards from my game Versailles 1919, co-designed with Mark Herman (Herman and Engelstein, 2020).

This is the alpha version of an Issue card. The game is about the negotiations around the Treaty of Versailles at the end of World War I. Each Issue card represents one of the discussion points at the conference and is the heart of the game. Figure 5.2 shows the alpha version of the Rheinland card, when the rules had stabilized.

Each Issue card shows several options that the player who wins the issue may select. The icons below each option show what impact that has on the world situation. For example, if the Rheinland remains with Germany,

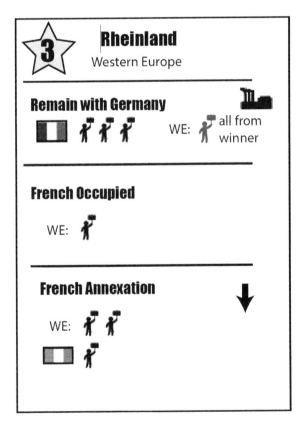

FIGURE 5.2   Versailles 1919 alpha-version card

France gains three Unrest (indicated by the French flag), and all Unrest is removed from the Western Europe region (shown by WE). The Industry icon shows that the world economy is helped by this decision. The header shows the point value of the card in the star (3 points in this case), and the Region is shown below the name (Western Europe).

This card layout was good enough to test everything. However, it caused a number of issues. First, the issues are laid out on the board, and we found that it was hard for some players to see the icons clearly from a distance. They needed to be larger.

In addition, players acquire a tableau of these cards in front of them, which could be as many as nine or ten. They took up a lot of space on the table, and we wanted things to be a bit neater, as players also needed space for their influence cubes, military tokens, and other assorted game markers.

After quickly iterating through a variety of layouts, we ended up with the design shown in Figure 5.3. To allow for larger icons, we went for a Tarot-sized card, which is 2.75″ × 4.75″, as opposed to the original 2.5″ × 3.5″ Poker card. We also rotated it to be in landscape orientation, to give more room for the options to breathe and to add the sidebar.

The grey sidebar worked out very well. This served two purposes. First, it helped to graphically separate the title and other information from the important options. Second, it allowed the cards to be overlapped in the

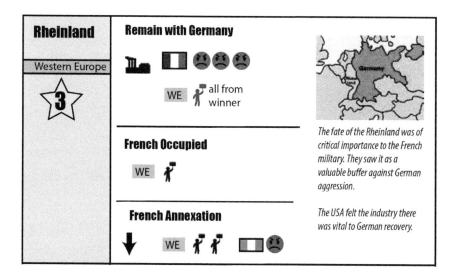

FIGURE 5.3   Versailles 1919 beta-version card

player's tableau, as after they are resolved, only the sidebar information (points and region) is important. We actually show in the rules how to overlap the cards to save table space.

This isn't a feature that changes the rules or is even strictly necessary. But it heads off a potential negative player experience, feeling that the game takes up too much table space.

In addition, this layout allowed us to include an illustration and historical context that increased the immersion and educational content.

Figure 5.4 shows the final production card. While I did the layout for the card in Figure 5.3, this one was done by an artist who actually knows what they're doing – Domhnall Hegarty. You'll note that the basic layout of the card was preserved from our beta set. In my experience this is very common. If you have put in the work to ensure a smooth play experience, the publisher's graphic artist can use that as a scaffold to build on.

You will note that the image and historical context were eliminated. This was done after a lot of discussion. We really liked the flavor that they imparted. However, eliminating them opened up additional space for us to make the icons even larger, which improved the usability even further. We did include the historical notes in the rules. It wasn't ideal, but we decided to err on the side of playability, which I don't think is ever a mistake.

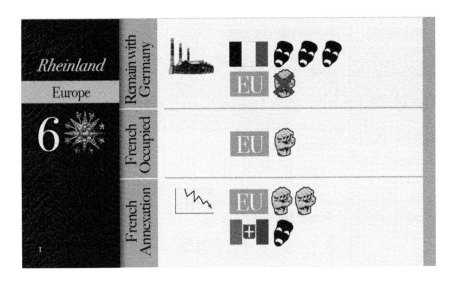

FIGURE 5.4   Versailles 1919 production Card

BETA DESIGN RESOURCES

When you're improving the art and graphics for beta, the resources listed in Chapter 2 will be very useful. Specifically:

- Icons

- Fonts

If you want to start including artwork, you have several options. If you are planning on self-publishing, this is a good time to begin commissioning final art and incorporating it into your prototypes. If you are planning on licensing to a publisher, you may also consider this. However, note that it is very unlikely that the publisher will use your art. They may have a very different artistic vision than you and will most certainly want to use their own design team.

An alternative is to use art from the internet, which is acceptable if you are simply making a handful of physical playtest sets. If you are posting anything online, or creating a virtual playset (see below), you should only use artwork that is properly licensed and attributed. Adding "royalty-free" in your search phrase can help in this regard.

BETA COMPONENTS

In addition to improving the graphic design of your prototype, this is an opportunity to increase the production values and sturdiness of your components. If you are going to be showing the prototype to publishers, or testing or demoing it at cons, having a more durable copy will pay dividends.

Many of the tips on creating components in the previous chapter apply here. However, there are some specific additional things you may want to do.

Tokens and Player Mats

Through most of alpha, simply using index cards and cardstock for tokens and player mats will be sufficient. As you move into beta and things are stable, consider using the "label on chipboard" approach described in the previous chapter. This will give you durable and easy-to-use components.

Boards

If you used a print shop to create your board as a poster, now is a good time to produce a laminated version or mount onto rigid backing material like foamcore. Mounting onto a rigid material may make it unwieldy to transport, so you might want to break larger boards down into smaller pieces.

Miniatures

If your commercial production will include miniatures, there are a few options for your beta prototype.

The first, and simplest, is to not worry about it and just use whatever you were using in alpha. Standees are a great substitute for miniatures if only a few are in your game. The previous chapter discusses in detail how to create standees for your game.

If you are planning on licensing your game to a publisher, almost certainly they will want to design their own custom miniatures if they decide to include them. Therefore, like art, investing in sculpting and prototype miniatures may not be the best investment of your time. As an alternative, if you want the table presence that miniatures can provide, you can either steal miniatures from other games or purchase ones that closely match the characters you have in mind. Reaper Miniatures has a tremendous variety in their reasonably priced Bones minis line (www.reapermini.com/miniatures/bones), for about $5 each, but there are plenty of other online resources.

If, by chance, I have not yet dissuaded you from incorporating custom miniatures, or if you plan on self-publishing and want to commission miniatures at this stage, then read on.

The first step in realizing a custom miniature is creating the geometry. The best free option for this is the 3D modeling package Blender (blender. org). Blender is incredibly powerful software that can be used to create stunning models and animations. That it is completely free and open source is, frankly, mind-blowing. An overview of Blender is well outside the scope of this book, but there is a myriad of resources available, including YouTube tutorials, books, reddit groups, and more, which will help teach you how to use this powerful tool. Fortunately, for creating miniatures you can focus on the geometry creation tools and safely ignore material creation, animation, lighting, special effects, and other advanced features.

Once your model is complete, you can use 3D printing to create the physical model. If you don't have access to a 3D printer, you can use online services like Shapeways (shapeways.com) and Xometry (xometry.com) to outsource your printing. You will need to export a file in STL format from your modeling software to send to the printer or service.

A 3D printer creates a part by slicing it into a series of horizontal layers and "drawing" those in plastic material. Because of this method there are limits to the resolution of features. Anything that is smaller than the size of a layer, or the diameter of the plastic filament, will get washed out.

Small features will be much crisper with actual molded parts. However, the molding process imposes constraints on your design that it are worth understanding at this stage, so you don't inadvertently make your miniatures much more expensive, or even impossible to produce.

Plastic miniatures are created through a process called Injection Molding. Plastic is melted and shot under pressure into a metal mold. The plastic cools and solidifies, and then the mold is opened, and the part is removed from the mold (*ejected*).

Molds are constructed in two halves, with an opening between them where the plastic is injected. Figure 5.5 shows a cross section of a mold that might produce a cup. The two halves of the mold can cleanly open up, leaving the part behind.

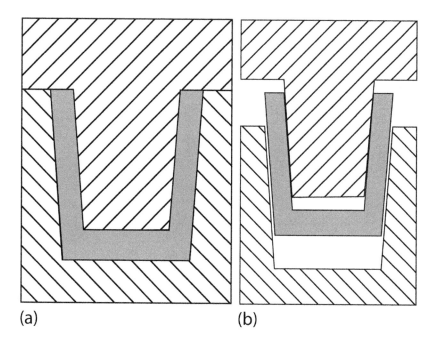

(a) (b)

FIGURE 5.5   Cross section of an Injection Mold for a cup

Let's say we want to add a handle to the cup. Now, if we try to open the mold the way we did before, the handle is stuck onto the metal. This is typically called an *undercut* (Figure 5.6).

There are a few ways to deal with this situation. First, the handle could be redesigned to be open on the bottom (Figure 5.7). Or, the mold can be designed with additional moving parts (called *slides*) that move out of the way as the mold opens, or when removed by hand. These add cost and complexity to the molds. Finally, an operator may be able to manually pull the part out of the mold depending on the flexibility of the plastic and how large the undercut is.

More complex miniatures may even need to be molded in separate pieces and assembled either at the factory or by the player.

As you are designing your miniatures, keep in mind how they are going to be ejected from the mold. If you don't, you may have some unpleasant surprises when you submit your miniatures to a manufacturer.

FIGURE 5.6   Injection Mold for a cup with a handle. Metal is stuck inside the handle

FIGURE 5.7   Handle with a partial handle to allow mold to open

ONLINE PROTOTYPING SERVICES

Another option for improving the quality of your prototype is to use an online prototyping service. These services allow you to upload files for cards, boards, punchboards, and other game elements and have them professionally printed. You can use these services for the entire game, or just select elements like a deck of cards.

The oldest of the online services is The Game Crafter (www.thegame-crafter.com), which began in 2009. Unlike the other services, The Game Crafter is not just a prototyping service, but also hosts games that people can order on a "Print and Play" basis. The games are only printed as they are ordered, and the designer gets a percentage of each sale. The Game Crafter also hosts Component.Studio, which was discussed in Chapter 1. Files created in this software can be automatically transferred to The Game Crafter for printing.

Other companies offering prototype production services include Print & Play (www.printplaygames.com), Superior POD (www.supe-riorpod.com; POD stands for *Print On Demand*), BoardGamesMaker

(www.boardgamesmaker.com), and Cartamundi (https://cartamundi.
com/en/make-my-game/).

Each of these has different advantages and ways of submitting your
design. For example, when submitting card decks to Print & Play, you
will download a template for the full sheet of cards and place your images
onto that. With The Game Crafter you will upload individual card faces,
and The Game Crafter will assemble the sheet for you, but requires very
specific pixel counts for each image. Poker size card images, for example,
must be exactly 825 × 1125 pixels. Spend a little bit of time reviewing each
site to see what the best fit is for you and your project.

All of the online prototyping services offer templates that can be freely
downloaded. These will lay out required safe zones, bleed, and die marks.
We will go into all of these in detail in the next chapter, but for now know
that these are production considerations which you need to take into
account when doing your component design. Even if you do not plan on
using these services, having these templates will help you make informed
decisions that will make the transition to commercial printing much
smoother.

VIRTUAL PROTOTYPES

Another option for beta prototypes is the use of virtual board game simu-
lators. These are programs that allow you to create, test, and play games
completely on a computer without physically making any components.
These programs were all developed with players in mind – with a way
to create virtual ways for people to play games together. But designers
learned, particularly during the COVID-19 quarantines, that they could
be used to create playtest sets as well as facsimiles of finished games,
increasing the number of people that could try prototypes.

Before getting into the pros and cons of using these tools, let's take a
closer look at the top three: Tabletop Simulator (TTS) (tabletopsimulator.
com), Tabletopia (tabletopia.com), and Vassal (vassalengine.org).

Tabletop Simulator and Tabletopia are similar in concept – create a
three-dimensional playing surface that emulates as closely as possible the
feel of sitting around a table. You can rotate the table and zoom in and
out. Everything happens in a single 'play space', such as holding a hand of
cards or placing reference cards on the table (Figure 5.8).

One of the main differences between them is the cost structure. Tabletop
Simulator is a one-time cost of $20. They do also charge for some game

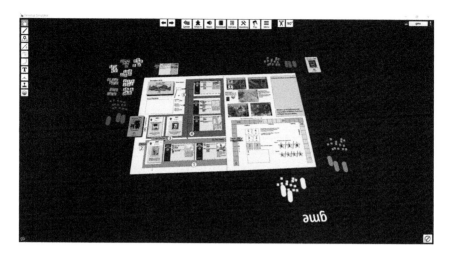

FIGURE 5.8   Tabletop Simulator for beta testing Versailles 1919

FIGURE 5.9   Tabletopia

implementations, but that doesn't apply to developing your own games. However, each of your players will need to own a copy.

Tabletopia is free for designers on a limited basis (if you only have a single project), with a monthly cost for more advanced use.

Both are available on Windows and Mac, through Steam, with Tabletopia also being available on iOS and Android (Figure 5.9).

Vassal originated as a way to help people play Advanced Squad Leader. The original name was VASL, short for Virtual Advanced Squad Leader. Eventually the tool was expanded to be usable for any game. Vassal is free and open source.

Vassal is different from Tabletop Simulator and Tabletopia in that it is a 2D "top down" tool only. You see the board, cards, and game pieces from an overhead view. There is no three-dimensional table view. Pieces and cards can be stacked on the table, but they are layered on top of each other.

It is also a windows-based program (small w, here). The board, your hand, and reference cards – each is in a separate window. This makes it easier for you to drag and set things up the way you'd like. But it also doesn't closely mimic the same feel as sitting around a table. In addition, the three-dimensional programs also implement a form of physics, so objects fall down, dice can be "physically" rolled, etc. If that is important to your project, Vassal will not work (Figure 5.10).

Another feature of these programs is scripting. Scripting basically lets the module developer attach a small program to a button or to certain areas of the table that automate activities. For example, if you have a card "river," you can have a button that automatically slides cards down and fills the end. The way that these programs handle scripting varies and depending on your eventual usage may be an important factor to consider when settling on a tool. However, scripting features are not that useful for

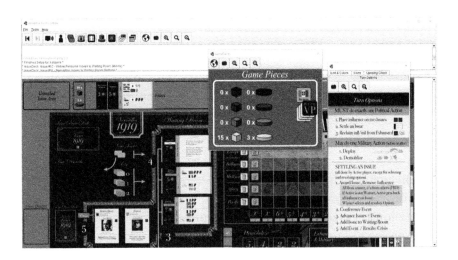

FIGURE 5.10 **Vassal**

prototyping, as they just add extra time to set up the module, to automate a process that will probably change anyway.

For this reason, we will not be going into the details of scripting here. However, keep in mind that this feature exists, and if you think you may want to use these tools to deploy polished modules after design lock, scripting may be an advanced feature to examine.

Virtual Prototype Example

Frankly, none of these programs were developed with the designer in mind. They are player centric and are filled with features that make the players' lives simpler. However, these features also make the creation of game modules quite complex, and all of these programs have a steep learning curve and are filled with annoyances for the designer.

All of them are actively being updated, but at the time I am writing this, Tabletop Simulator is a bit less complex and is the tool of choice for more developers. Again, "tool of choice" in this case means the lesser of evils. None of these tools are intuitive or straightforward.

To give you a flavor of the process of using one of these tools, let's walk through creating a board and deck of cards in Tabletop Simulator (TTS). The full range of any of these programs is well beyond the scope of this book, but this should give some idea of the process.

To start, you will need to prepare your files. For the board and tokens you can just output a JPEG or other image file.

Cards are a bit more complex, as they need to be in a specific format. Cards need to be laid out in a grid, with up to ten columns and seven rows. In each grid cell you will place the image of one of your cards. If you have multiple copies of a single card, it should be included multiple times in the grid. If you have more than 70 cards, you will need to have more than one card grid file.

You can use your graphics program of choice to create the grid, or you can create individual card images and assemble them into a single sheet using a Deck Builder tool that is included with TTS.

To get to the Deck Builder, you will need to find out where TTS is installed. The simplest way to do this is go to into Steam, find Tabletop Simulator in your Library, right-click on the entry, and select Properties. From the form that is brought up, select the Local Files tab, and then click on the Browse Local Files button. That will open a window to the TTS files. You will see a directory called Modding, in which is another folder called Deck Builder, where the program is located.

The first time you do this, you might consider creating a shortcut to the tool, so you don't need to go through this each time.

A sample card grid is shown in Figure 5.11.

Once you have all of your image assets ready to go, you need to make them accessible to TTS via a URL. There are several ways to do this. If you have Dropbox on your computer, you can use Dropbox links. Otherwise, you can upload the files to Imgur, Google Drive, or other service that can give you a link to each file. Dropbox is great to use because if you update the file with new graphics, but save it in the same location and same name, the URL will stay the same and Tabletop Simulator will automatically update the game set the next time you open it.

Now that everything is in an internet-accessible location, we can begin to assemble our game module. To do this:

- Launch Tabletop Simulator.

- Select Create>Single>Classic>Custom. This will create a basic setup for you with a table, board, and a few pawns. You can customize those, or if you want to create them from scratch, delete those items. Then select Object from the menu on top of the screen and then select CUSTOM. You can then create the custom Deck and Board object from there.

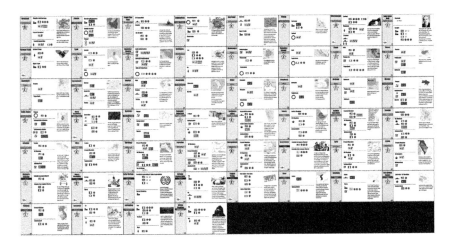

FIGURE 5.11   Card grid for Tabletop Simulator

When creating a custom card deck, you will first place the deck and then see the form shown in Figure 5.12, which has a variety of options.

Type lets you switch the basic shape of the card. Typically you will want Rectangle (Rounded), but you can also make hexagonal or circular cards.

Face is where you enter the link to the file you created earlier with the grid of cards. If you are using Dropbox, it may look something like https://www.dropbox.com/s/2qizrdctkzosvk0/1919%20Issues.png?dl=0.

(IMPORTANT: When pasting this into the box, make sure to change the dl = 0 at the end to dl = 1. Otherwise the linking will not work properly. This is just an issue with Dropbox. If you are using Imgur, you don't need to worry about this.)

The file for the **Back** can either be a single image (if all backs are the same) or a grid of images, like the card faces, if each card has a

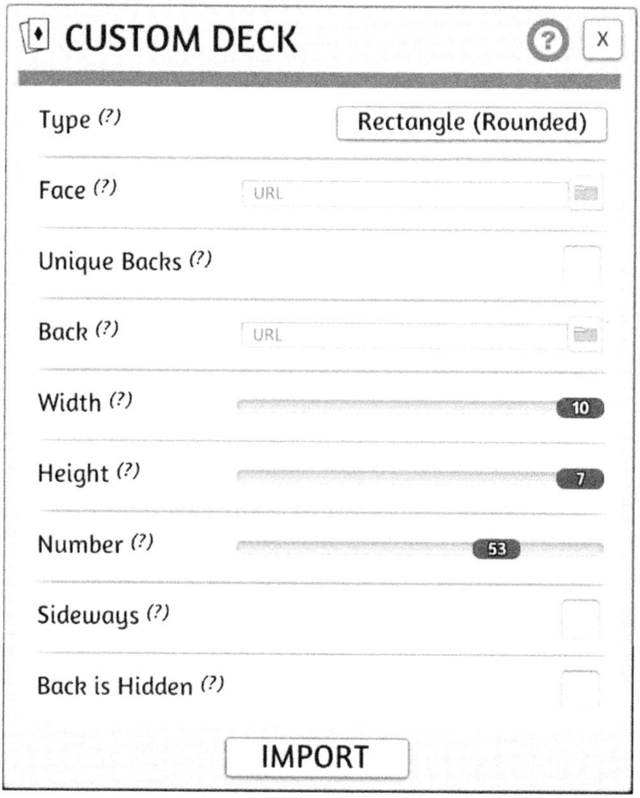

FIGURE 5.12 Import Card Deck dialog

FIGURE 5.13   Import Board dialog

different back. If you do have unique backs, make sure to check the Unique Backs box.

The **Width** and **Height** settings tell TTS the grid that your cards are broken up into. In the figure you'll see that it's set to 10 × 7, which is the largest the grid can be, at 70 cards.

The **Number** field is how many of the cards are filled. For example, in the Versailles card sample image shown in Figure 5.11, the grid is 8 × 7, but there are only 52 cards. The last four card spots are black, and we don't want those turned into cards. So we would put 52 into this box.

The other settings are for non-standard setups, and you can explore those as needed.

If everything has worked according to plan, when you click the IMPORT button your card deck will appear on the table.

To make a custom board, all you need to enter is the URL for the graphics (Figure 5.13).

Once you bring the element in, you can scale it as required to fit the table and the other components.

When you have everything setup, click Upload under Upload Workshop. This will store it into an initially private area on Steam. The first time you do this the project will be given a Workshop ID. In the future if you update the project you may want to use the same Workshop ID. Just enter it in the Update Workshop form and click Update (Figure 5.14).

Tabletop Simulator Tips

Here are some additional tips for designing with TTS:

- Blocks, chips, and other standard components are already in the Object library in TTS. You can scale these and set the colors to create a variety of game components.

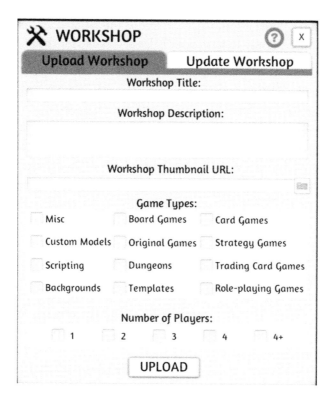

FIGURE 5.14   Workshop dialog

- Bags are particularly useful. They come in two flavors: *Normal* and *Infinite*. Normal bags can hold different types of objects, and you can randomly draw or specifically select items out of them. They are also great for keeping the table tidy, to hold unused tokens and such. Infinite bags only hold one type of object, but it can be drawn infinitely. They are good for coins or other tokens where there is no limit to how many can be in the game.

- The ALT key zooms in on whatever the mouse is over.

- You can set up multiple camera views to, for example, quickly switch between a view of the main board and your player mat. You can also set up a "picture-in-picture" that shows two camera views simultaneously.

- When setting up the maximum number of players, leave it at ten (the limit). This way you can include observers, such as yourself, to just watch the action.

- TTS can import a multi-page PDF file and show it as a component. This can be handy to have your rules accessible for the players.

- By default, Mod Caching is on. This means that if you change an image file (like your card deck file), the next time you open TTS it will *not* load the new file. It will just use the saved one. This makes loading faster, which is why it is the default. But during development you typically want this option off to make updating your playset faster. To turn off Mod Caching, click on the Menu icon on the top menu bar and select Configuration, and you will see the Mod Caching checkbox.

Virtual Prototyping Pros and Cons

The pros of using a virtual prototyping tool are obvious. It may take a little longer to get setup the first time, but once you are set, and you get the hang of using the tools, it can be much faster to update components as opposed to printing, slicing, sleeving, mounting, and all the other techniques we have been discussing. It is also less costly, as you don't need to buy toner or cardstock.

In addition, it's easier to get a playtest game going. You don't need people in the same room, and your pool of potential players is much larger.

However, there are definite downsides. First, there is what designer Gil Hova calls "The Tabletop Simulator Tax." This isn't a monetary tax – it's a time tax. It takes longer to play a game with any of these virtual tools. When you are at a table you can very quickly grab a card, place a tile, and you have two hands to work with. Plus, it's easier to grasp the entire board state and then take a closer look at a particular spot in real life than it is with a virtual tool.

Everything just takes more time – estimate 50%–100% more time. And if everything takes longer, player engagement will drop, and you won't get as good a read of how it's really playing.

While this isn't a book about playtesting, I will give another playtesting tip. For me, perhaps the most valuable part is simply watching the body language of the players. I know some designers that have lengthy post-game questionnaires for the players, for example. And while talking to your playtesters is important, players don't always remember where they got tripped up, or what they misinterpreted, or how many times they checked their phone during a game.

When doing a virtual playtest, that entire channel of information is gone. It is basically impossible to gauge player interest in the same way. Perhaps you can run more playtests, but you are going to get a lot less information out of each.

Also, personally I find that the physical acts of me, as the designer, pushing pieces around, stacking things, and generally playing are very important factors to being creative and getting new ideas. I have yet to really come up with new and creative thoughts while playtesting online in the same way I do when I'm physically pushing things around. This is, obviously, more of an issue during early stage alpha testing. But it is still something to consider.

Like all tools described here, you should use what works for you. There are also tools that, while specifically designed for role playing games, like Roll20 (roll20.net), may also be useful depending on the nature of your game. I think a blend of physical and online prototypes will probably become the standard method for designers in the future, using each to its strengths.

CHAPTER 6

Production

Y OUR DESIGN IS COMPLETE, fully playtested, and ready to be released to the world! Now you need to supply the materials to the production house to turn it into reality.

When preparing for printing and manufacturing, there are certain details that you need to be cognizant of. While each manufacturer will have their own preferences, this chapter contains common elements that you should be aware of. We will also review typical costs of common components. Understanding these issues earlier in the process will help avoid some nasty surprises when you send your project out for quote.

PRINTING CONSIDERATIONS
Bleed and Margin

No manufacturing process is perfect. When cutting cards, for example, the cut will be at a slightly different place each time. When molding plastic, the dimensions will vary slightly for each part. The amount of variation you can expect is called the *tolerance* of the process, and it is important to plan for that in your layout.

Two ways of compensating for tolerance in printing are *bleed* and *margin*. *Bleed* is the part of your artwork that extends beyond the actual size of the component. When punchboard is cut, for example, the cut may vary slightly for each sheet. If your artwork just extended to the expected cut line and stopped there, you would notice when the cut is slightly off. By extending the background art beyond the nominal size, and to the edge of the tolerance, you know that even as the cut varies your background will look consistent.

Margin is the flip side of bleed. If key information in the component runs all the way up to the cut line, like text, if the cut line shifts your text may be (literally) cut off. Adding a margin to the inside of the card that has no key information means that even in a worst-case cut shift your key information will still be visible. This is why the margin lines define what is sometimes called a *safe zone*. Anything inside the safe zone will always be on the component (Figure 6.1).

Color

Most printing is done using what is called *process color*. Process color uses four colors – cyan, magenta, yellow, and black – and creates other colors by blending these. Because of the colors used this is called the CMYK

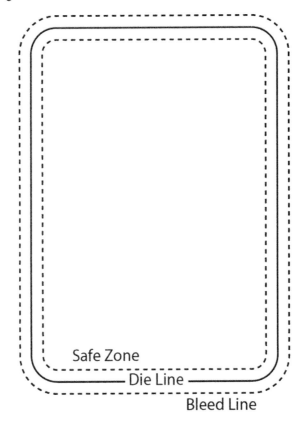

FIGURE 6.1   Sample bleed and margin regions for a card

process. When printing, there will be a separate plate that prints each color onto the page.

Another option for color printing is called *spot color*. In this process, rather than blending colors together to form the desired color, you have a specific ink of the color you want and a plate to print that. Spot color can produce more vibrant and precise colors but is typically only used if there are just a few specific colors on the page.

Most game printers are set up for a CMYK process and not spot color. However, it is good to be aware of the option.

Most graphics software will allow you to work in a CMYK color space. Make sure you are set to that rather than RGB. You can convert from RGB to CMYK, but working in that space from the start means your colors will most closely match your intention (Figure 6.2).

When working in CMYK, more sophisticated software packages will ask for a *Working Space* to use. Selecting the proper Working Space will ensure the most accurate reproduction of your colors. Currently the most globally used standard is FOGRA 39. Adobe products default to US Web Coated (SWOP), so make sure this is set properly (Figure 6.3).

Black is the New Black

The "K" part of CMYK is a pure black ink. It is used for a few reasons. First, blending 100% of Cyan, Magenta, and Yellow doesn't produce a true black. It's close, but the eye can tell the difference.

FIGURE 6.2   Image Mode menu in Photoshop

Coated FOGRA27 (ISO 12647-2:2004)
Coated FOGRA39 (ISO 12647-2:2004)
Coated GRACoL 2006 (ISO 12647-2:2004)
Japan Color 2001 Coated
Japan Color 2001 Uncoated
Japan Color 2002 Newspaper
Japan Color 2003 Web Coated
Japan Web Coated (Ad)
U.S. Sheetfed Coated v2
U.S. Sheetfed Uncoated v2
U.S. Web Coated (SWOP) v2
U.S. Web Uncoated v2
Uncoated FOGRA29 (ISO 12647-2:2004)
US Newsprint (SNAP 2007)
Web Coated FOGRA28 (ISO 12647-2:2004)
Web Coated SWOP 2006 Grade 3 Paper
Web Coated SWOP 2006 Grade 5 Paper

FIGURE 6.3 Available color spaces in Photoshop

Also, the different inks are applied in different steps, and like all manufacturing processes, there will be a slight tolerance in where they are placed on the page. For small, precise features like text, your eye will notice the slight offset between colors and register it as blurry. Having a single black pass will make sure your text is crisp and legible.

A true black in CMYK space is 0%, 0%, 0%, 100% – in other words, 100% black ink, and none of the colors. Text and other features, like icons, that you want to be black and crisp should be defined as true black.

However, for artwork, borders, and other features where crispness is not as critical, it can sometimes be good to add other inks to your blacks. This is known as a *rich black*, and it can make your black look more vibrant and lustrous. Different graphic designers and printers will have their own recommendations for the formula for a good rich black, so check with them when finalizing the artwork.

Exporting Graphic Files

Graphics files should be created at 300 ppi (pixels per inch) or higher and submitted to the printer as PDF files. Most printers will have their own preferred settings on how to receive the graphics files, so check with them.

For example, typically cards will be submitted with a single card on each page, with a separate file for fronts and backs. Others will want fronts and backs merged into a single file.

Die lines (drawings showing cut lines for punchboard, for example) are also submitted as PDF files. However, color profiles and other fine details are not critical on these, as they are just schematics showing where cuts should be made.

Three-dimensional data is typically submitted as STL files. The name STL comes from the word "Stereolithography," which is an early technical term for 3D printing. You will want to output with as fine a resolution as the 3D creation software allows, to give smooth surfaces. Otherwise you may see facets across large curves.

Cards are printed on sheets and then cut to size. Here are the typical numbers of cards per sheet:

Size	Cards per sheet
Poker (2.5″ × 3.5″)	54
Tarot (2.75″ × 4.75″)	32
Mini-Euro (1.75″ × 2.75″)	84

It's a good idea to keep the number of cards per sheet for your chosen card size in mind while getting into the final stages of your design. The amount that you pay for cards is based on the number of sheets that are required per game, not the number of cards.

For example, if you're using Poker-sized cards, including 40 cards in your game will cost the same as 54. But going from 54 to 55 cards will incur a huge cost bump, as the game will now require two sheets, with just a single card on the second.

If you have extra spaces for cards on your sheet, consider adding reference cards or even advertisements for other games you may have made or have coming up. Or design a few additional abilities or cards if possible.

Printers may have their own sheet sizes that vary from the ones listed here, so check when making these final decisions. And, of course, you are not limited to these sizes. All printers can create cards of any size, but an unusual size may incur a setup charge.

When cards are cut, there is a single blade pass in between the cards. So, the left side of one card is the right side of its neighbor. This means that ideally the color or pattern that is on the edges of the cards needs to match – specifically the area from the margin to the end of the bleed. If not, you may get thin stripes of color or image which do not look good.

Let's take a look at two cards to illustrate this. Let's say you want one card to have a white background and one to have a gray background. Figure 6.4 shows them arranged next to each on the sheet.

Notice how the white and gray are up against each other on the cut line? In order for those cards to come out the way you want, the cut must happen precisely on that boundary. But as discussed at the start of this chapter, all manufacturing processes have some tolerance, and the cut will frequently not be precisely on that boundary.

Figure 6.5 shows what happens if the cut is slightly to the right. The white card will have a stripe of gray on the right side, which is not the look you want.

To avoid this issue, all cards should have the same border color. Typically, this is black, although different printers may have different preferences. If you look at cards from Magic: The Gathering, you'll see that they all have this black border. This is one of the reasons why (another being that you can't tell the identity of cards from the side of the deck).

If you want to have cards with different borders on the same sheet, there are a few tricks you can use.

One option is to group cards with like color borders together and have the blank cards in between the blocks. We used this technique in my game The Fog of War. The mini cards were printed on a large sheet of 224 cards.

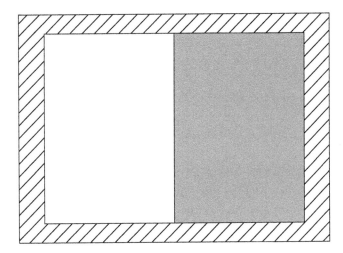

FIGURE 6.4   Adjacent white and gray cards on a sheet

FIGURE 6.5   Cut card. Offset cut results in gray stripe on right

This was more than we needed, so we took advantage of the extra space to bring the color all the way to the edges of the cards rather than add a neutral border. The resulting sheet is shown in Figure 6.6.

If you want true full bleed cards, with artwork running all the way to the edge that you don't want on the adjacent card, you can go with double-cut cards. This process leaves a strip of unused material between each card. It gives maximum flexibility but is slightly more expensive.

Localization

Printing is typically done with a four-plate process – one plate for each of the colors in the CMYK model. However, some printers will have a fifth plate. This is most often used for localization – changing the language for different target markets. Card titles, effects, and other language-specific items can be placed on this last plate. This minimizes the number of changes that need to be made to manufacturing in order to localize. Since it's just a single plate, it can only do one color, most commonly black.

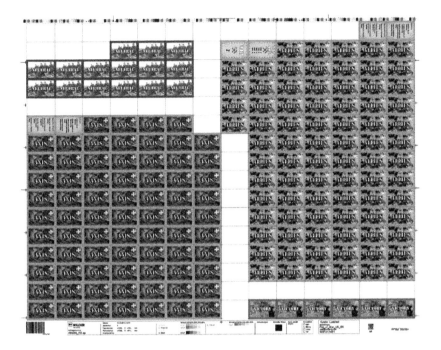

FIGURE 6.6   Fog of War card sheet. Each of the large blocks has its own unique background color

If you have white text on a black background you won't be able to use this fifth plate technique. It will still be possible to localize but will take more effort. Having black text will give you the most flexibility, although adding a fifth plate will increase setup costs. As always, reviewing options with your printer before committing to a course of action is recommended.

Card Materials

There are several different types of base material that can be used for your cards. Like cardstock and other papers, they are typically rated as being a certain *gsm*, which stands for *grams per square meter*. It is the weight of one square meter of the paper.

Different cores will also have different flexibility, snap, and "shuffleabil-ity" (we'll see if the editor lets that word go). Higher grade cores will feel more solid and will be more durable.

- Gray core (lightweight): 275 gsm

- Blue core (normal): 300 gsm

- Ivory core (premium): 310 gsm

- Black core (deluxe): 310 gsm

As a reference, casino cards are typically black core. Magic: The Gathering cards are blue core.

Note that different manufacturers have different names for these. Requesting samples and gsm ratings is a good thing to do to ensure you are getting what you think you are getting. Also, if you ask a manufacturer to quote on "blue core" cards, for example, and they don't know what that means, that's a bad sign.

Card Options

There are a variety of different card finishes, including matte, gloss, and linen (going from least to most costly). You can also upgrade cards with metallic inks, foil printing, or other techniques to give them a little extra pop.

PUNCHBOARD

Many game components can be created with punchboard, including tokens, coins, player boards, standees, reference cards, and more. We'll talk about some of the more esoteric items in the next section, but here we will focus on some core considerations for designing punchboards.

Die Lines and Safe Zones

Punchboards are created by laminating paper on two sides of a piece of chipboard. A metal cutting die is then built that stamps out the pieces. Typically, pieces are left in the frame and included whole in the game for the purchaser to (gleefully) punch out.

Like all processes, there are manufacturing tolerances in both the printing and cutting processes. Therefore, you should include 3 mm of bleed outside of the die line to compensate for misalignment. You should also keep a safe zone of 3 mm inside the die line to make sure that no critical information is cut off during the punching process.

Figure 6.7 shows a sprue from Caverna: The Cave Farmers (Rosenberg, 2013) which clearly illustrates the use of bleed around each token. The black line inside each block of color is the die line where the punch die has pierced the punchboard.

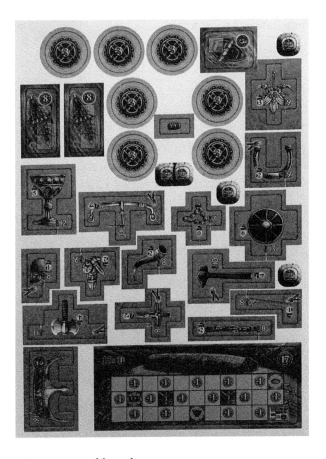

FIGURE 6.7   Caverna punchboard sprue

The coins in Figure 6.8 shows what happens if your artwork has a pattern that goes all the way to the edge of the die. The circle is clearly off-set here, showing the tolerance of the punch. In this particular game, the coins are supposed to have a rustic, ancient look, so it does not detract from the aesthetics. But that choice should be made with eyes open. If there had been no pattern around the outside and no inner circle, it would have masked the off-center punch.

Distance between Cuts

Punchboards almost always contain more than one token. You should leave at least 6 mm (about 1/4″) between adjacent tokens or between a token and the edge of the sheet. This will prevent tearing of the

FIGURE 6.8   Coin tokens showing offset punch

punchboard during cutting and handling. If there is a long, straight edge between tokens you may consider leaving even more space.

Single Cut between Two Components

To pack more tokens into a sheet, you may have two tokens touching each other and separated by a single cut. If you do this, there are a few considerations.

First, you need to make sure that they share the same background color. The cut will never be precisely where you want it, so the cut area needs to be a single color or pattern.

Second, a token can never be completely surrounded by cuts and not attached to the main frame at some point. If you try, the punchboard will tear during manufacturing. Wargames came with token frames similar to Figure 6.9. The groups of two rows are typical of wargame counter sheets. They are done this way so that every token has at least one edge connected to the frame. If you have three or more rows, there will be some tokens that will be isolated in the center of the block and not cut properly.

Reusing Dies

You will need to pay for each unique die in your game. An 11″ × 11″ die is about $500. If you have multiple token sheets, it will save you money to make as many of them the same as possible. One trick you frequently see in games is to spread different components onto different sheets. For example, let's say you have a game that has 15 small rectangle tokens,

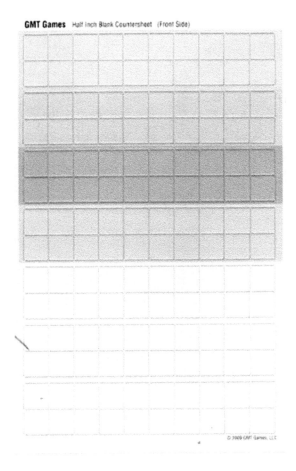

FIGURE 6.9 Typical wargame counter sheet. Tokens are arranged in rows of two to ensure they remain attached to the punchboard sprue

15 circular coins, and 9 large rectangles. One option would be to make three sheets – one with the small rectangles tokens, one with the coins, and one with the rectangles (top of Figure 6.10). This will require three dies and cost $1,500.

However, by rearranging the pieces, you can save a lot of money. If you put 5 squares, 5 coins, and 3 rectangles onto each sheet, you now only need a single die, used three times. Your die costs are reduced from $1,500 to $500.

Thickness

Standard punchboard thickness is 2 mm. Depending on needs, you can go thinner (1 mm or 1.5 mm) or as high as 6 mm. My game Survive: Space

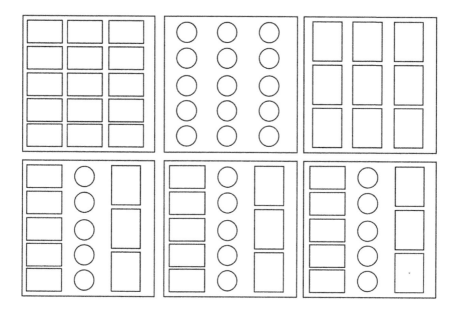

FIGURE 6.10   Two different punch die arrangements. Top row = $1,500 tooling, bottom row = $500

Attack had hexagonal tiles that ranged from 2 mm to 6 mm in thickness, which created a neat multilevel effect when the map was built by the players.

Upgrades

Like other printed components, you can upgrade your punchboard with spot UV, foil, metallic inks, and other features. You can also have the manufacturer pre-punch the items for you to save space or give a more professional presentation.

PUNCHBOARD CONSTRUCTIONS

A few years ago, I was talking with the owner of a game production company and asked him what he thought the most underused game component was. His reply, surprisingly, was punchboard. Which is weird because almost every game has some sort of token sheet included.

But he clarified that he was referring to "Punchboard Construction" – using punchboard to build 3D game pieces, structures, and other game features.

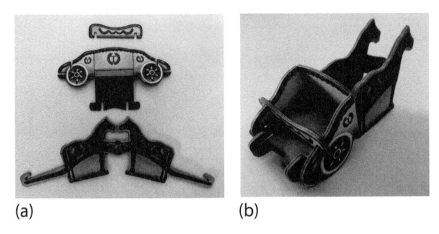

(a)   (b)

FIGURE 6.11   Chariot pieces (a) and assembly (b) from Tribune. Chariot car is slightly separated to show the assembly detail.

You see this more frequently now – the trees in Photosynthesis (Hach, 2017), marble rack in Potion Explosion (Castelli, Crespi, Silva, 2015), the large tree in Everdell (Wilson, 2018), and submarine in UBOOT (Pluta, Salwarowski, 2019) all take advantage of this technique. But it is still something that can add excitement and table presence to your game and get it noticed. At the 2018 Gencon game convention, the towering tree of Everdell did a great job attracting crowds.

The best technique for attaching two pieces of punchboard is a 90-degree half-slot joint. The two pieces you want to connect each contain a slot that mates with the other. Figure 6.11 shows the pieces that make up a chariot in Tribune: Primus Inter Pares (Schmiel, 2007). Using only three pieces with cleverly placed scoring to allow the punchboard to flex, the players can create a visually arresting chariot as a centerpiece for play.

The slot width should be the same as the thickness of your punchboard. This will give a nice snug fit.

If possible, your box should be designed to hold the assembled pieces. Each time you assemble and disassemble the structure you weaken the joint, as the slots get slightly larger each time.

GAME BOARDS

The guidelines for game boards are quite similar to those for cards and punchboard. A few points are worth mentioning.

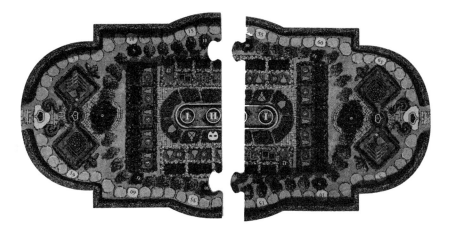

FIGURE 6.12   Puzzle Board from Noblemen (Sullivan, 2012)

First, the bleed will need to be much larger than a card or punchboard – 18 mm is typical. This is due to the way that the paper wraps around the edges of the board core.

Second, printing on the back of the board adds very little cost. You should strongly consider having a double-sided board, perhaps to offer different play experiences or to accommodate different player counts. At the worst case, you can always create some decorative artwork.

Finally, consider where the board will be broken up when it folds. If possible, design your artwork so that the folds lie in the least obtrusive area and don't go straight through numbers, for example. While alignment for cuts and folds is good for boards, if possible, it is best to try to shift things away from joints where possible.

Templates for different size boards showing folds can be found at several game printer websites, such as Panda Games.

An option for traditional folding boards is a Puzzle Board. These are made of punchboard and are assembled as a jigsaw puzzle. They are typically less expensive than folding boards (Figure 6.12).

GAME BOX

While there are some games that ship in a reclosable bag, most likely you will want to ship your game in a box. There are two types of boxes. By far the most common is the *two-piece box*, which has a top and a bottom. The other is a *tuckbox*, which is typically used for smaller card games and is similar to the box a traditional deck of cards comes in.

Most printers will be able to supply you with a template for laying out your box artwork, which will include bleed – typically 15–20 mm – and die lines. The die lines for boxes can be tricky, so it is best to get them from your printer rather than lay them out yourself. Note that the bleed is much larger than that which is required for cards, as the paper will wrap around the edges of the box, requiring more margin.

Protip: If you are doing a two-piece box, there are several sides that are often left blank or with very basic artwork, including the outer sides of the box bottom and the insides of both cover and bottom. These are great places to put artwork with a fun surprise or other information for the player. The outside of the box bottom is particularly good, as adding artwork here doesn't cost anything additional, since it will be printed along with the main box bottom. If you want to print on the insides of the top or bottom there will be an additional cost (Figure 6.13).

If possible, you should use a standard box size, for two reasons. First, players and retailers appreciate having a standard box size, as it makes the games easier to sell. Second, if you use a custom box size you will have to pay tooling charges for the dies to create the box, which typically cost about $750 depending on size. Your printer will advise which sizes they already have tooled up.

However, if a custom box is best for your project, then go for it. Sometimes having a smaller custom box will save on freight costs, which, depending on the size of your print run, can offset the extra tooling charge.

FIGURE 6.13   Versailles 1919 box bottom showing printing on outside surfaces

The thickness of material in a game box ranges from 1.5 mm to 2.5 mm. The 2.5 mm boxes are noticeably sturdier but will be more expensive. Other options you might consider for your box are to line the interior and print on it or add spot UV (shiny spots to highlight certain parts of the artwork), foil stamping, or embossing (raised sections).

Game boxes should have certain markings. Some are required by law, some are required to sell the product in a store, and some are information for the consumer.

- **Country of origin:** This is required if you will be shipping the product across international borders, so most likely you will need it. It can be as simple as "Made in <country>."

- **Age range:** This serves two purposes. For the consumer, this is informational and lets them know the intended audience. However, it also has legal ramifications. If a game is intended for children 13 years old or younger, it is classified as a toy and requires certain safety markings.

In Europe, toys must meet the EN-71 standard. You will need to include the CE logo, with a minimum height of 5 mm. You also must include applicable warning icons or text, along with a description of the hazard.

In the United States, toys are covered by ASTM F963. It requires similar warning text and iconography as EN-71.

Figure 6.14 shows a typical marking on a game box.

If your game is intended for people aged 14 or older, it is not a toy. No safety markings are required.

FIGURE 6.14   Typical box markings (UPC/EAN code to be printed in white box to the right)

Note that these requirements are revised over time, and this book reflects regulations as of early 2020. You should always confirm that there have been no updates to the regulations when designing your packaging.

UPC/EAN code: While not required by law, retailers and distributors will require that your game have a bar code. A bar code has a unique company prefix and a product ID. The company prefix is assigned by the GS1 organization, which maintains a standard database.

If you don't want to go that route, there are online brokers that sell individual bar codes that will have their company prefix. However, there are less-than-reputable sellers that reuse bar codes for different customers and other shenanigans that may result in your product being pulled from Amazon or Walmart, for example. So, don't always go for the lowest cost.

BOX INSERTS

Often when you open a new game you will see a cardboard insert. This is called a u-channel insert, or a valley insert (Figure 6.15).

FIGURE 6.15 Cardstock valley insert with printing

Some people believe the purpose of this insert is to provide storage for the game pieces in between plays. Most often this is not the case. The purpose of this style of insert is to take up empty space below the punchboards, boards, and other large components to ensure that they remain safely in place and do not rattle around during shipping and handling.

This is another opportunity for custom printing and decoration that only adds a small amount to the cost of production.

It is possible to use cardboard to create a more functional custom storage solution, but it requires a multi-piece assembly. As an example, Stone Age (Brunnhofer, 2008) includes the four-compartment insert shown in Figure 6.16. This supports the components during shipping as well as providing a storage solution after the pieces are punched out. It is formed by two separate cardboard pieces – one larger piece, creating the pockets and short divider, and a divider piece.

For actual storage solutions, some games include vacuum-formed trays. These are manufactured by warming up a thin sheet of plastic and then sucking it down over a metal form, shaping it. The vacuum is cut off and the plastic releases from the forming die and is trimmed, creating the final tray.

Because of the process, there can be no undercuts (overhangs) in the tray. Everything needs to be "in the line of draw" so that the plastic can be pulled vertically off the die. You cannot, for example, have tabs that stick out over a pocket to hold things in place. If you wish to hold things firmly, the best approach is to have vertical ridges that create a friction fit.

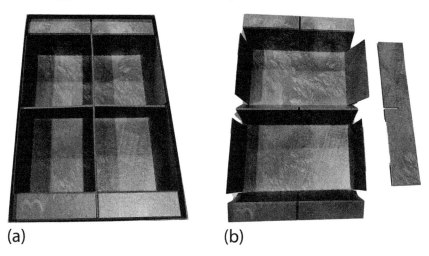

(a)   (b)

FIGURE 6.16 Stone Age cardboard storage insert: (a) assembled, (b) unassembled

You can also create nested pockets, so that a smaller item goes deep in a pocket, and then there is a larger item on top of that (like a deck of cards, for example) and then a larger token on top of that. The plastic will take on the look of an inverted ziggurat, keeping each component in its own zone.

In addition, because plastic shrinks as it cools and the way it is pulled from the metal die, side walls need to have an angle on them called "draft." The exact amount of draft and other features (like corner radii) to prevent tearing and ensuring proper fit and function is usually best left to engineers that are familiar with this process.

Be prepared for there might be multiple iterations of tooling required to get the precise fit you desire. Usually slight adjustments to the tooling to tweak the size of the tray are required, and the overall process can take 12 weeks. Make sure to leave time for that in your schedule so that the production of the tray is not holding up the entire project.

A nice touch to include on tray inserts is a guide to show where everything should go. This can either be printed in the rules, on the inside of the cover, or through raised letters on the tray itself. An example of this is shown in Figure 6.17, with the name of each character indicating the area for those components. The empty tray on the right also has nested concentric circles for King Arthur and Sinbad (upper left, lower right) that are for

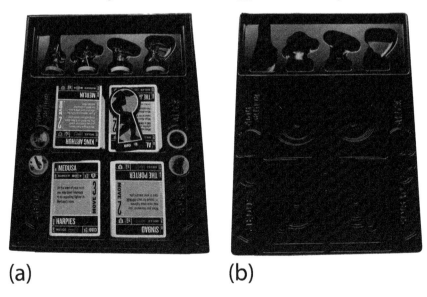

(a)   (b)

FIGURE 6.17 Vacuum-form tray from Unmatched (Daviau, Honeycutt, Jacobson, 2019), (a) with components and (b) without.

multiple dials. The smaller dial is placed first, with the larger on top. This tray also shows effective use of finger slots in the disc areas, making it easy to remove these components.

MEEPLES

The term "meeples" originated as a shorthand for referring to the wooden people tokens in Carcassonne (Wrede, 2000), as a contraction of "my people" or "mini people." While the people shapes are the most common, there are now bewildering arrays of custom meeple shapes that have been included in games.

These silhouette wooden figures are formed by creating a wooden stick with the right profile and then slicing the stick into individual components. Because these are created through a computer-controlled process, the possibilities for creating intricate shapes are endless. The more intricate the shapes, the more they will cost, but these are not expensive components.

Basic shapes are generated through a mechanical machine-cutting process. More complex and detailed shapes need to be done with laser cutting, which increases costs. Details about costs are given later in this chapter.

Custom-shaped meeples can add a lot of flair to a production without much additional cost (Figure 6.18).

To take your meeples to the next level, you may consider printing on the faces. This is a nice upgrade for a Kickstarter exclusive or for a deluxe version of the game. Figure 6.19 shows a gas tank, gun, brick, and worker for the game 51st State (Trzewiczek, 2010).

STORAGE BAGGIES

As an alternative to a vacuum-form tray insert, or in addition to it, you can also include baggies to hold components. If your budget permits, I highly recommend including some reclosable bags (often known under the commercial name of *Ziploc bags*), particularly for games that have a lot of pieces. Your players will appreciate it, and the easier it is to set up and tear down your game, the more likely people are to play it.

Reclosable bags are available in a vast array of sizes, so you should be able to get a size that works for you. It's easiest if all bags are the same size,

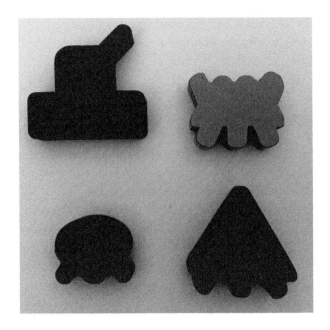

FIGURE 6.18 Detailed meeples from Survive Space Attack

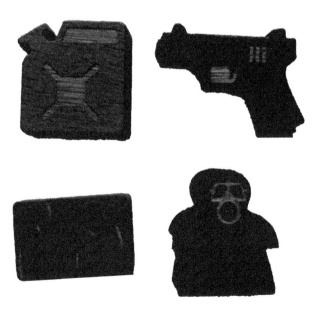

FIGURE 6.19 Meeples with printed details from 51st State

but you can have a larger size for card decks, for example, and smaller ones for cubes.

RULES

Rules are submitted to the printer as PDFs. Each individual rules page should be a page in the PDF. Do not create two-page spreads as a single page. The printer will organize the pages into the proper booklet format. A bleed of 3 mm is usually sufficient, although for certain quantity and size of page, it may need to be larger.

If your rules are more than just a single sheet, they will need some type of binding. By far the most common is a Saddle Stitch binding. The pages are attached by two staples along the seam. Saddle Stitching requires that the number of pages in your rules will need to be a multiple of four. If you have excess space after laying out your rules consider adding additional examples of play, reference guides, design notes, or advertisements for other games (Figure 6.20).

Saddle Stitch binding is limited to about 48 pages depending on the exact equipment. More than that, then the pages don't stay together properly and are difficult to close.

Another common binding is Spiral Binding. Similar to the notebooks many of us used in school, Spiral Binding for games is typically done with a plastic coil. Spiral Binding needs a page count multiple of two.

The advantage of this type of binding is that the rules can lay flat when placed on the table. Some games actually use pages of the rules to play on, such as Quirky Circuits (Valens, 2019) and Jaws of the Lion (Childress,

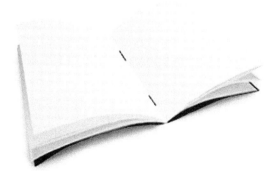

FIGURE 6.20   **Saddle Stitch**

FIGURE 6.21   Jaws of the Lion scenario book. Spiral Binding allows the book to lay flat. Photo courtesy of Isaac Childress

2020). In the game shown in Figure 6.21, the pages are actually the boards, so laying the pages flat is critical.

In addition, Spiral Binding can go to a much higher page count than Saddle Stitch, so you can see it in large sourcebooks like Tales of the Arabian Nights (Gallela, Goldberg, Maroney, Shlasinger, 2009). Also, frequently, the front and back covers are a heavier cardstock, to improve durability.

The two other commonly used bindings are Perfect and Casewrap. These are comparable to paperback and hardcover books, respectively. You frequently see these types of bindings with source books and supplements, particularly in the world of role-playing games. These books are often sold independently in bookstores and are stored on shelves.

MINIATURES

The design and production of miniatures is discussed at length in the previous chapter. The cost of miniatures is probably the most variable item discussed in this chapter, both in tooling and piece price. It is important to review your design with your manufacturing partner, as they can be invaluable in giving you advice to keep costs down.

FIGURE 6.22 Pre-painted and washed versions of the same miniature from Navia Dratp (Yamazaki, 2004).

Most miniatures are shipped assembled but unpainted. However, to save cost, you can ship the miniatures on the sprue and have the customer cut them out and/or assemble them prior to play. This is typically done for miniatures-based games like Infinity and Warhammer, but mainstream consumers are not ready to assemble miniatures when they open a game.

Many manufacturers can pre-paint miniatures for you. As you can imagine, this can add a lot of additional cost depending on the quality level and detail of the miniatures and the paint job. If you think you may want pre-painted miniatures, be sure to discuss it as early as possible with your manufacturer. If they need to pre-paint, it may change the way that the miniatures are molded or assembled. So make sure they are aware of this.

A nice compromise between unpainted and painted miniatures is to add a wash. This is a thin, dark liquid that is used to coat the miniature. It will settle in the cracks, making deeper areas look darker, and raised portions brighter. A wash is an easy way to give your minis some pop (Figure 6.22).

DICE

Dice can be obtained in a dizzying variety of shapes and styles. The least expensive approach is to use standard dice. But if you have custom icons on your dice, there are several options.

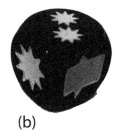

(a)　　　　　　　　(b)　　　　　　　　(c)

FIGURE 6.23　(a) Pad-printed die and (b) engraved die. (c) Full color pad printing was used in the dice for Star Wars: Destiny (Konieczka, Litzinger, 2016).

First, the symbols can be pad-printed onto the sides of the die. This can be done in a single color or multiple colors, like any printing process. It is the least expensive way to get a custom die, but also may rub off over time. If the die is not used that much, then a printed die is fine. We used this type of die in Survive: Space Attack, as it is only rolled one time per turn.

The other option is engraved dice. In this process an indented symbol is put into the side of the die and then filled with enamel or ink. Because the symbol is recessed, these dice are very durable. However, a custom tool needs to be built to mold the dice, and this can be costly.

We used this type of dice for Space Cadets: Dice Duel, since the dice are constantly being rolled. Durability was paramount (Figure 6.23).

TYPICAL COMPONENT PRICES

Component prices will vary based on many factors. However, it is useful for the designer to have an idea of component costs, even if you are planning on licensing your design. I reached out to Panda Games (pandagm.com), and they graciously provided price range information on a wide variety of components. This should be used to get an idea of price ranges. Ultimately it may be higher or lower, and prices may vary over time based on raw material prices and economic conditions, and different manufacturers have different pricing. If the precise pricing is important for your project (which it obviously will be if, for example, you are planning a Kickstarter), you should obtain quotes on your specific project.

All of the prices below are for 5,000 units. Here are approximate multipliers if you are looking at different quantities:

Quantity	Multiplier
2,000	1.25

5,000	1.0
10,000	0.9

For example, a two-piece box is about $1.50 at 5,000 piece quantity. If you order 2,000 pieces, the price would be approximately $1.88 ($1.50 × 1.25), and at 10,000 pieces it would be $1.35 ($1.50 × 0.9).

Some items have tooling charges. These are one-time costs to build the tools, dies, and fixtures required to produce the component.

Component	Quoted Specification	Price
Two-piece Box	295 mm × 295 mm × 70 mm 2 mm thick	$1.40–$1.60
Cardboard Insert	Custom fit to box 300 gsm cardstock One compartment, no print	$0.30–$0.33 $150–$250 tooling
Custom Vac Tray	1.3 mm PVC plastic Black Copper mold	$0.85–$1.00 $450–$650 tooling
Rulebook	216 × 279 mm 128 gsm gloss paper 8 pages	$0.09–$0.11
Poker Cards	63 mm × 88 mm 300 gsm blue core 54 card deck Shrink wrap	$0.45–$0.55
Mini Cards	44 mm × 67 mm 300 gsm blue core 84 card deck Shrink wrap	$0.55–$0.65
Gameboard	560 mm × 840 mm 1/6 fold 2 mm thick Wrapped edges Reinforced folds	$1.65–$1.85 $200–$300 tooling
Punchboard	280 × 280 mm 2 mm thickness 1 die cut	$0.27–$0.39 $400–$500 tooling

(Continued)

Component	Quoted Specification	Price
Sticker Sheet	279×216 mm 80 gsm sticker sheet 1 die cut Gloss varnish	$0.22–$0.24 $100–$200 tooling
Cardboard Mats	279×216 mm 400 gsm Matt varnish	$0.16–$0.27 $0–$500 tooling depending on shape
Polybags	85×120 mm PE plastic Transparent, resealable	$0.10–$0.16 for 5
Wood Cubes	8×8×8 mm 4 unique colors Set of 20 (5 of each)	$0.25–$0.35
Wood Discs	13 mm diameter×3 mm 4 unique colors Set of 8 (2 of each)	$0.10–$0.16
Standard/Simple Meeples (machine cut)	16×16×10 mm 4 unique colors Set of 4 (1 of each)	$0.12–$0.18
Complex Meeples (laser cut)	16×16×10 mm 4 unique colors Set of 4 (1 of each)	$0.20–$0.27
Custom Plastic Minis	1 miniature	$0.09–$0.20 $3,800–$5,200 tooling
Plain white D6, standard pips	16 mm	$0.08–$0.10
Pad-printed Die	16 mm	$0.15–$0.25
Engraved	16 mm	$0.15–$0.25 $2,500 tooling
Other Costs	Assembly Shipping cartons Pallets	$0.70–$0.80

If you are planning on self-publishing, you will need to select a manufacturing partner. An internet search will turn up a wide variety of companies that do game manufacturing. Designer Rustan Håkannson maintains a list at https://boardgamemanufacturers.info/. Joining game designer groups on Facebook, reddit, Discord, and other platforms can also give you insights into what others have experienced with different manufacturers.

Game manufacturers are also starting to exhibit at game design events like Unpub as well as game conventions like Essen Spiele and Gencon.

SHIPPING AND DISTRIBUTION

Another cost to evaluate will be shipping to your warehouse, whether that is your own warehouse, distributor, or fulfillment center. Getting your game into distribution, Kickstarter fulfillment, and other logistics considerations are beyond the scope of this book. However, there are a few costs that you want to make sure you understand if you are putting together a self-publishing business plan:

- Freight to your warehouse

- Import duties (if producing in another country)

- Distribution/fulfillment costs

- Kickstarter fees

- Credit card fees

Your manufacturer will be able to assist you with estimating freight costs. However, in general, if you are bringing product into the United States from overseas, the most efficient way is using ocean freight to ship a full 40' *container* of product. A "container" is a standard metal shipping container that you see on a tractor trailer. If your game is about the size of a Ticket to Ride box ($300 \times 300 \times 70$ mm), about 7,500 units will fit in a 40' container if they are floor loaded and about 5,500 if they are on pallets. You can certainly ship any amount, but the shipping costs will be the most economical if you ship a full container. For example, it costs about $4,500 to ship a 40' container from China to the United States and about $3,000 for a 20' container, which holds half as much.

Thanks again to Panda Games for providing this benchmark pricing. Remember that these prices are rough estimates and will vary. Please make sure to get actual quotes to prepare for a Kickstarter or any business planning.

CHAPTER 7

Conclusion

THERE ARE SEVERAL THEMES that run throughout this book that should govern your development process. I'd like to once again emphasize them here, to underscore their importance.

INVEST YOUR TIME WISELY

There's no roadmap or direct path of how to get from A to Z when designing a game. As a creative process, there will be lots of fits and starts, and lots of discarded material. On a purely practical basis, the less time you spend on ideas that don't work, the faster you will reach your goal.

But there is a psychological element as well. Decades of research into human psychology has shown that the more we invest time in something, or simply have it in our possession, the harder it is to let it go. And yet design is about being able to discard ideas, mechanisms, and designs that just aren't working. The more time you invest in an asset or a mechanism, the harder it will be to move on when it isn't working – or even worse, when it's good but not great.

STICK WITH YOUR TOOLS

There are dizzying arrays of tools available for every task, with more being released every day. They all have strengths and weaknesses. However, in my experience, it is better to stick with one tool rather than jump back and forth between different ones. Even if another tool is a bit better at the specific task you're now doing, the time you take to learn a new tool will eliminate any efficiency advantage.

Of course, you need to keep an eye out at new tools, both software and physical, and see if the new kid on the block is sufficiently advanced over your current tool to make the switch. In the process of researching this book, I discovered several tools that I have since adopted into my work-flow. But I did not make the decision to move lightly. I know many people that like to flit between different tools and use something for a month or two before jumping to the *next big thing*.

You'll be better served by committing and moving on when there are clear advantages.

FOCUS ON USABILITY

As a designer you are crafting an interactive experience for your players. Make sure that they get the most out of that experience by making the graphic design clear and supporting the players as much as possible. Fonts should be readable, icons clear, and colors differentiated. You don't need to be an artist to accomplish this. Attention to detail and watching your players will be sufficient to get you 90% of the way before bringing in a professional graphic designer for the home stretch.

Your graphics should not get in the way of the players playing the game. Speaking of which …

RULES ARE A BARRIER

Rules are the original sin of tabletop games. Video games have worked hard to eliminate as much of the barrier as possible to just playing the game and learning as you go. You should do everything in your power to make the game easy to understand and play. This starts with the design itself, as you eliminate rules exceptions, and things that work counterin-tuitively. But it continues with graphics design, as you add signifiers and affordances, and actually writing the rules.

Use hierarchies both in the rules and in the graphic design to guide the player to what's important. Start with a high-level view and then gradually drill down into the details.

Remember that the rules need to be both Rules as Tutorial and Rules as Reference. Depending on the scale of your game, there are a variety of ways to approach it, but always keep this in mind. Don't skimp on using a rules editor, and if you can, make sure to conduct a few blind playtests.

DON'T SWEAT THE DETAILS, THEN SWEAT THE DETAILS

Throughout this book I have emphasized rapid iteration. That often means that you will ignore the fine details of graphic design and rules layout. As you progress through the design, however, they should increase in importance in your thinking. The balance of how much to worry about the details and when will come with experience. But keep in mind that you should neither obsess over details early on nor leave all of them for the last minute. Gradually change your focus.

MAKE THE PROCESS YOUR OWN

For every piece of advice I have given in this book, I know of someone who works differently. Each person has their own approach that works for them. But just like learning any skill, there are a set of best practices that should be learned. Then, as you gain experience, you will see what works for you and what different approaches you would like to take. Ultimately this is about establishing a process, and every person will have different strengths and weaknesses and different motivations and obstacles.

HAVE FUN ALONG THE WAY

Designing a game is a long process. The average game takes about a year to develop, and then once it is in the hands of the publisher, takes another one or two years before it reaches the market. It can be a frustrating journey with many twists and turns.

And yet, it can also be a rewarding one. Game design is an intriguing blend of creativity, psychology, and engineering that touches many aspects of the human experience. As a designer your goal may be to bring a certain period in history to life, give players a puzzling challenge to overcome, teach a skill, or simply provide some escapism. Whatever the goal, watching players embrace the experience you have prepared for them is tremendously fulfilling.

RESOURCES

Here is a list of internet resources relating to prototyping and producing games, arranged alphabetically within each category.

Communities

- Board Game Designers Forum (BGDF): www.bgdf.com

- Cardboard Edison: https://cardboardedison.com/

  Cardboard Edison is a fantastic aggregator of board game design resources. They also run an annual design contest.

- Card & Board Game Designers Guild Facebook Group: www.facebook.com/groups/GameDesignersGuild

- r/tabletopgamedesign Reddit Group: www.reddit.com/r/tabletopgamedesign/

Components and Prototypers

These are discussed in detail in Chapter 5

- Board Games Maker: http://boardgamesmaker.com/

- Cartamundi: https://cartamundi.com/en/

- Print & Play: www.printplaygames.com

- Spielmaterial.de: www.spielmaterial.de

- SuperiorPOD: www.superiorpod.com

- The Game Crafter: www.thegamecrafter.com

General Graphics Software

- Adobe: https://creativecloud.adobe.com/

- Affinity: https://affinity.serif.com/en-us/

- Blender: www.blender.org

- GIMP: www.gimp.org

- Google Draw: https://docs.google.com/drawings

- Inkscape: https://inkscape.org/

- Microsoft Office: www.office.com

- Scribus: www.scribus.net

Game-Specific Software

- Campaign Cartographer: www.profantasy.com/products/cc3.asp
- Component.Studio: https://component.studio/
- Inkarnate: https://inkarnate.com/
- Hexographer: www.hexographer.com
- NanDECK: www.nand.it/nandeck/

Virtual Tabletops

- Tabletop Simulator: www.tabletopsimulator.com
- Tabletopia: https://tabletopia.com/
- Vassal: www.vassalengine.org

Icons

- Flat Icon: www.flaticon.com
- Game-icons.net: https://game-icons.net/
- Open Icon Library: https://sourceforge.net/projects/openiconlibrary/
- The Noun Project: https://thenounproject.com/

Fonts

- DaFont: www.dafont.com
- Font Squirrel: www.fontsquirrel.com
- Fontello: http://fontello.com/
- IcoMoon: https://icomoon.io/

Color Blindness Testing

- Chromatic Vision Simulator: https://apps.apple.com/us/app/chromatic-vision-simulator/id389310222
- Color Oracle: https://wearecolorblind.com/resources/color-oracle-color-blindness-simulator/
- Toptal: www.toptal.com/designers/colorfilter

Manufacturing

- Board Game Manufacturers Info: https://boardgamemanufacturers. info/

Podcasts

- Board Game Design Lab: www.boardgamedesignlab.com
- Board Games Insider: http://boardgamesinsider.com/
- Breaking into Board Games: https://breakingintoboardgames.libs yn.com/
- Ludology: www.ludology.net
- Meeple Syrup Show: http://meeplesyrupshow.com/
- On Board Games: https://onboardgames.libsyn.com/

INDEX

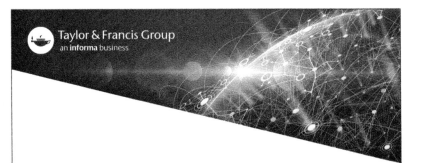

Printed and bound by CPI Group (UK) Ltd, Croydon, CR0 4YY

24/10/2024

01778301-0002